REMBRANDT'S HOLLAND

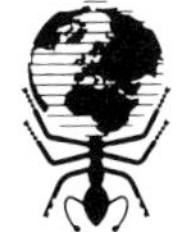

Books in the RENAISSANCE LIVES series explore and illustrate the life histories and achievements of significant artists, rulers, intellectuals and scientists in the early modern world. They delve into literature, philosophy, the history of art, science and natural history and cover narratives of exploration, statecraft and technology.

Series Editor: François Quiviger

Already published

REMBRANDT'S HOLLAND

LARRY SILVER

REAKTION BOOKS

Published by Reaktion Books Ltd
Unit 32, Waterside
44–48 Wharf Road
London N1 7UX, UK
www.reaktionbooks.co.uk

First published 2018
Paperback edition first published 2024

Printed and bound in India by Replika Press Pvt. Ltd

A catalogue record for this book is available from the British Library

ISBN 978 1 78914 873 2

COVER: Rembrandt, *The Syndics of the Drapers' Guild*, c. 1662, oil on canvas. Rijksmuseum, Amsterdam (on loan from the City of Amsterdam), reproduced by kind permission

CONTENTS

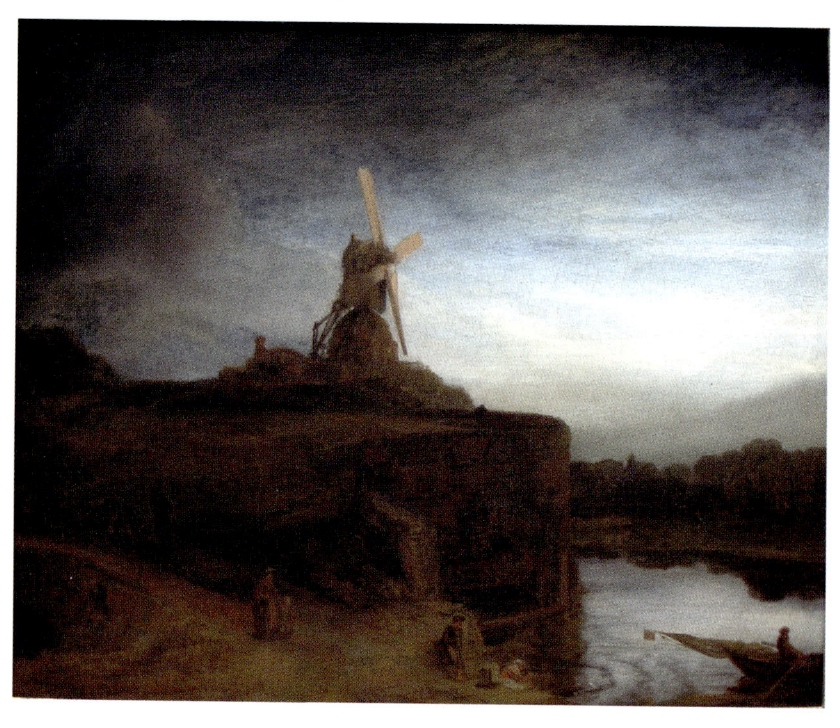

Preface

REMBRANDT BOOKS FILL almost an entire library, from full-scale life-and-works studies that take a comprehensive view of his entire career, to detailed study of individual works or the artist's techniques as a painter, draughtsman or printmaker. Good popular books, both well written and well researched, also exist about the artist. So why write another one, and how will it differ from earlier introductory studies?

First a little personal background on credentials. My own experience with the artist extends across a career, now in its fifth decade, of scholarship and teaching. My graduate adviser, the late Seymour Slive (1920–2014), was an acknowledged dean of Rembrandt studies of his generation, so I had authoritative early exposure to Rembrandt and his century. As for a track record, almost three decades ago I wrote an entry on Rembrandt for the *Encyclopaedia Britannica* (1988 edition; recently replaced) and then an introductory essay for a popular series by Rizzoli (1992). But I also co-authored a massive study, years in the making, with a distinguished colleague and Rembrandt specialist, emerita professor Shelley Perlove, *Rembrandt's Faith: Church and Temple in the Dutch Golden Age* (2009). It analyses the religious content of all of the artist's

1 Rembrandt Harmenzsoon van Rijn, *The Mill*, 1645–8, oil on canvas.

paintings and prints across his career against the contemporary background of Amsterdam's dynamic, shifting social and cultural setting.

In many respects this more modest and accessible volume grows out of that large, scholarly monograph. It, too, aims to situate Rembrandt in his cities and in his century. Predictably, most approaches to Rembrandt biography tend to look at him in isolation in a survey of his career by decades. Given the charge to write a brief biography of Rembrandt for the Reaktion series Renaissance Lives, I chose instead to show Rembrandt's interactions with his several environments – with the city of Amsterdam and her citizens (including those who did not patronize him), with the complex religious mix of that city as well as the wider nation (including the university theologians in his birthplace of Leiden), and even with the contemporary politics – particularly involving the ruling court of the stadholder in The Hague, whose support he sought, avidly at first, but ultimately in vain. Along the way, I have also tried to suggest some of Rembrandt's artistic models, particularly Peter Paul Rubens, but also a roster of celebrated Italian artists of the Renaissance and recently imported Caravaggism by way of nearby Utrecht painters of his youth.

While this survey begins with the necessary basics of biography, career and self-representation (Rembrandt was one of the most prolific artists ever of self-portraits), its later chapters also outline the history of his Dutch Republic, which achieved national independence during his lifetime after a long-term revolt. The artist's own religious and political beliefs remain difficult to determine with any certitude, but his serious engagement with such wider issues will comprise the main contours of the chapters that follow. His lifetime coincides with the official birth and the early national biography of the Dutch Republic, the modern Netherlands, whose largest and most prosperous province is Holland. Thus the name of this modest volume is dual: *Rembrandt's Holland*.

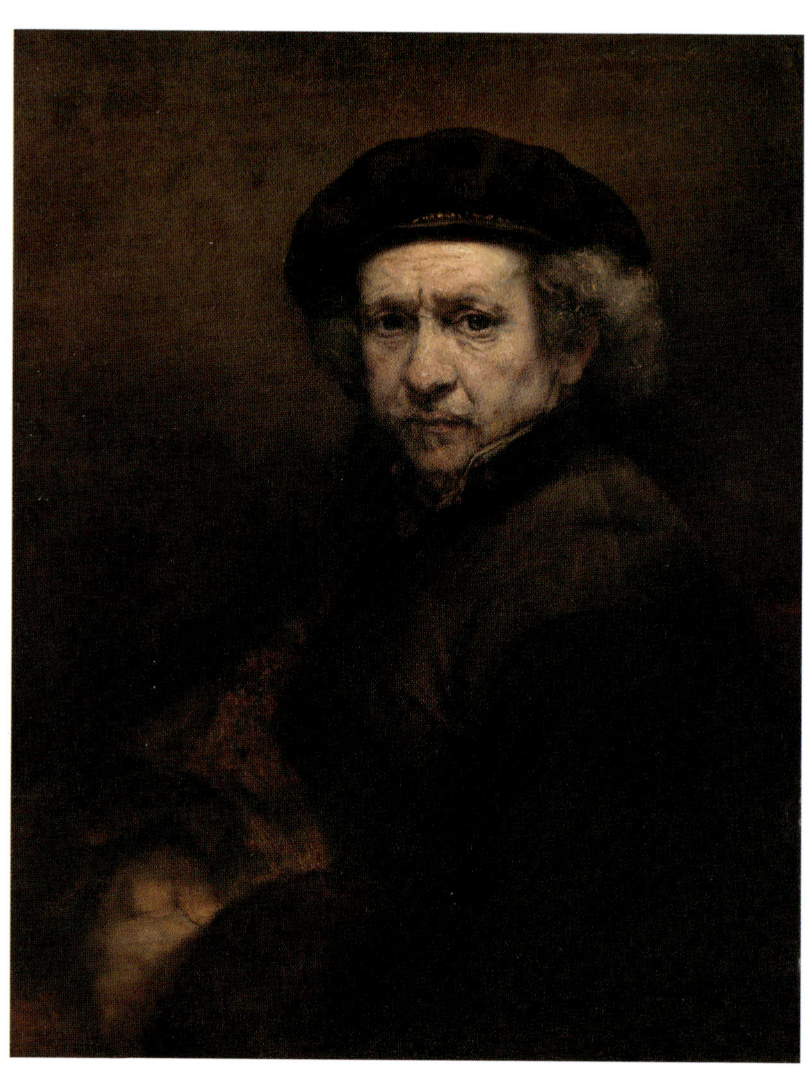

Stirrings in a New Dutch Nation

ISTORY CHANGED IN 1595, when a Dutch ship organized by Cornelis de Houtman successfully arrived in the East Indies at what had become known as the Spice Islands. Despite setbacks, that voyage returned with precious cargo in August 1597, across the entire Indian Ocean, around the Cape of Good Hope, and up the Atlantic, after it opened up Dutch claims to settlement on Java near the town of Bantam. Soon, more Dutch fleets would return with armed vessels to establish their own colonial trading post nearby, naming that new regional node on Java after their own legendary ancestral region, Batavia. Dutch ships already traded actively across Europe, reaching as far as Scandinavia and Russia, and, in their drive to rival established Portuguese routes to the fabled spice-growing regions of Southeast Asia, Dutch ships even ventured by way of a northern route, but were stymied in icy winter seas above Russia in Nova Zemblya.

De Houtman's return led directly to the formation of several private fleets in 1598, but in 1602 Johan van Olden-barnevelt, Advocate of Holland (1568–1618), organized those competitors into a state-sponsored monopoly, a pioneering joint-stock company, the Dutch East India Company (VOC

2 Rembrandt, *Self-portrait*, 1659, oil on canvas.

was the abbreviation of its Dutch name, initials that marked the goods of the Company). Already in late 1600 England formed the East India Company with its own charter from Elizabeth I. Soon VOC ships established a regular trade route to Asia with established fortified compounds along the way in such outposts as Cape Town, Colombo and Makassar, as well as Batavia itself. Eventually their routes featured an Asian triangle of trade: shipment of silver from Japan to China for silk and porcelain, then exchange of those goods for spices to return to Europe. In effect the VOC established a form of global commerce and consumption well before the modern era, and successfully introduced tea, coffee and 'china' porcelain to worldwide consumers.

Comprised of representatives of seven separate Dutch port cities, with burgeoning Amsterdam given a dominant role, the new VOC arrangement also reaffirmed the fragile alliance of separate provinces that was emerging as the Dutch Republic at the turn of the seventeenth century. What is now called the Dutch Revolt began in the 1560s as an independence movement from rule by the Spanish king Philip II. By 1568 harsh punishments of Dutch nobles by Spanish regents led to military resistance and all-out warfare in the greater Netherlands, modern Belgium and northern France. In its early years the Dutch Revolt was led by William of Orange (1533–1584), a high noble raised at the court in Brussels who held major government positions, particularly the title of stadholder (governor, literally lieutenant) of Holland, Zeeland and Utrecht, which became the leading provinces of the Dutch Republic. Though assassinated in 1584, William 'the Silent' became revered as the father of his country. The Dutch

Republic developed out of the original seventeen provinces of the Netherlands, split into two states by the military outcome of the Revolt, where a southern, still-Spanish entity (often called Flanders after its largest, most prosperous county; roughly identical to modern Belgium) separated from the remaining seven United Provinces (often called Holland after its most populous and prosperous province), established in 1579 by the Union of Utrecht. The definitive military break occurred in 1585, when Spanish forces led by Alessandro Farnese recaptured Antwerp and then governed the Spanish South Netherlands (r. 1578–92) but failed to advance farther north. A truce between 1609 and 1621 established de facto national boundaries, confirmed by the treaty of Westphalia at the end of the Thirty Years War in 1648.

The house of Orange remained ruling stadholders, chiefly military commanders, first under Maurits of Nassau (1567–1625), son of William the Silent, and then under his youngest brother Frederik Hendrik (1584–1647). Their court in The Hague determined the location of the parliament (or States General). In effect, the federal political structure of the new nation remained decentralized except for the military, leaving real power in the hands of leading cities and their merchants; as with the voc, both politics and trade were dominated by Holland, led by Amsterdam.

That political struggle also became tightly intertwined with movements for religious freedom, because Spain remained uncompromising in its commitment to the Catholic faith, but Dutchmen were increasingly attracted to Calvinist preachers and diverse other Protestant sects that arose during the sixteenth century. As early as 1566 petitions to end religious persecution led to systematic emptying from city churches of religious statues and painted altarpieces, a movement known as the *Beeldenstorm* (iconoclastic outbreak). The founding document of the Union of Utrecht assured freedom of conscience in the practice of religion in the Dutch Republic; moreover, after the fall of Antwerp in 1585 a large wave of immigrants – perhaps as many as 100,000 of them – from the South Netherlands fled northwards, often for religious reasons. Among them, Iberian Jews from both Spain and Portugal sought asylum in the Republic.

But Calvinism remained the leading religion in the new nation, led by the Dutch Reformed Church, and other religions were obliged to meet privately. Yet even among the Calvinists a major split occurred, prompted by theological disputes over the doctrine of predestination at the University of Leiden, founded in 1575 to train ministers in the Reformed Church. As a result, no official state religion was ever established in the Dutch Republic, although the Reformed Church was designated as the 'public church', and religious pluralism, particularly diverse among Protestant sects, prevailed in the new nation.

True toleration remained restricted by politics: Catholics had to follow their faith in virtual secrecy, and Jews remained second-class citizens by statute, although some Jewish merchants thrived through their connections to Portuguese and Spanish trade networks as importers of new consumer commodities, especially sugar and tobacco. In Amsterdam Jews also successfully managed to control their own community and they soon established a truly public presence without traditional medieval stigmas of required costume or badges. The first rabbi immigrated in 1602, and the first public synagogue opened in Amsterdam in 1612 – even receiving a visit from stadholder Frederik Hendrik in 1642. But the Reformed Church fully dominated public worship in the Dutch Republic, and the general European doctrine prevailed of a region following the religion of its ruler (*cuius regio, eius religio*).

Dutch independence was secured by its military, led by the stadholder. Its success in international trade was under-pinned by Europe's leading navy, which neatly overlapped with its merchant fleet. Already in the early years of the Dutch Revolt privateers, known as 'Sea Beggars', had successfully defended military gains on land, but the state began to take responsibility for ship-building. Victorious admirals remain a roll call of honour from seventeenth-century Dutch wars: Piet Heyn, Maerten Tromp and Michiel de Ruyter. Those heroes all are buried in elaborate carved church tombs, two of them near William the Silent in Delft. After mid-century Dutch naval supremacy was first tested, then bested in a series of Anglo-Dutch wars (from 1652 to 1654, and from 1665 to 1667), whose outcome ultimately established that 'Britannia rules the waves'.

The Dutch army was relatively small by contemporary European standards, and it initially suffered setbacks by Spanish invasions and sieges, notoriously those of Haarlem, Middelburg and Leiden (from 1572 to 1574; but also of Breda in the 1620s, after the Twelve Years Truce ended), which were ended by breaking dykes to use floods as additional defence. However, the Republic pioneered innovations in army disci-pline and tactics, especially under Maurits of Nassau. Instead of the larger units of the Spanish army, *tercios*, Maurits forces were smaller and tightly drilled in co-ordinated activities as companies. To ensure familiarity with the new standard-issue handgun firearms, Haarlem artist Jacob de Gheyn II produced a step-by-step illustrated manual, *Wapenhandelinghe* (The Exercise of Arms, 1607), about loading and firing the weapons, arquebus or musket, as well as spear-like pike. Corporate pride and collective action by a unit replaced the individual strength and valour of the medieval knight as military virtues on the battlefield.

Once the relative safety of the Dutch Republic was assured during the Truce (1609–21), a recurrent state of tension arose between the largest port cities (Amsterdam, Rotterdam and Dordrecht), whose merchant elites wanted peaceful conditions to pursue their international trade, versus the stadholders and the court in The Hague, who preferred war powers and military authority. Joining the Orange faction were other cities, led by Leiden and Haarlem, which had suffered during earlier invasions and worried about securing the borders and protecting their own textile production against free trade. Essentially federalism and free trade were opposed to protectionism, whether military or economic. The Republic's lack of central authority only promoted this ideological conflict of interests, which resulted in vacillating tensions, intensified at certain critical moments. Especially in 1618, when stadholder Maurice arrested and executed the political leader, Oldenbarnevelt, and also embraced the cause of the most orthodox Calvinists in their desire for a state religion, he dismantled the peace party for the moment and brought the Republic to the brink of civil war, only interrupted by the end of the Truce in 1621 and the wider European Thirty Years War.

During the third quarter of the seventeenth century, the Republic plunged into a leadership crisis soon after the death of Frederik Hendrik. First, his young son and successor William II (r. 1647–50), like Maurice before him a strong proponent of the war party and supporter of domination in the Republic by the strictest faction of the Dutch Reform Church, suddenly died. Real control of the government lay in the balance, and for a generation the cities and the peace party prevailed during what is called the 'stadholderless period', led by Grand Pensionary Johan de Witt of Dordrecht (1653–72), a figure like Oldenbarnevelt. At this moment, Amsterdam and Holland were at their apogee, a provincial authority with effective international standing with newly confirmed national independence and power after the conclusion of the internecine Thirty Years War.

Flush with confidence, Amsterdam built an enormous and magnificent City Hall in classicizing style, designed by Jacob van Campen, to replace the old structure, condemned in 1639 for demolition but burnt down definitively in 1652. The new City Hall, commissioned already in 1648, was dedicated with great fanfare in 1655, despite the interruptions of the first Anglo-Dutch War. Some Dutch triumphs were still to come on the military front, led by Admiral Michiel de Ruyter's daring rush up the Thames and into the Medway, towing away the English flagship and ending the Second Anglo-Dutch War in June 1667.

But war did ultimately close in on the Republic and on Johann de Witt when England allied with France under Louis XIV; their combined fleets attacked in 1672 and nearly overwhelmed the country and with it the relative autonomy of the separate cities and provinces. War with France extended across four more decades thereafter, and the domination of the peace party was crushed. Indeed, 1672 is known in Dutch history as the 'Year of Disaster'. William III was elevated to military leadership and the stadholder position last held by his father. De Witt resigned, but soon afterwards he and his brother were assassinated in The Hague on 20 August. Military collapse was accompanied by a stock-market crash on the Amsterdam Exchange and by a resulting loss of capital to London. Collapse of support for the arts was both immediate and widespread. In part as a defence of his own nation, William III married the English princess Mary Stuart in 1677, and through her he would eventually lay claim to the throne of England in the Glorious Revolution of 1688 in a reign (1688–1702) better known as that of William and Mary.

Dutch contributions to European civilization – evil as well as good ones – stem directly from this seventeenth-century history. New World slavery, unfortunately, owes much to Dutch commerce. Rivalry with the Portuguese in Asia was soon matched by competition across the Atlantic, and in 1621 (right after the Truce) the Dutch West India Company (WIC) was established as a counterpart to the VOC. Here admiral Piet Hein first made his name as a privateer, particularly after his 1628 capture of the entire Spanish silver fleet in Cuba. The WIC captured several Caribbean islands in 1634: Aruba, Curaçao and Bonaire, the modern-day Dutch Antilles. Brazil was taken from Portugal in 1630, and the Dutch set up a productive coastal colony there for fifteen years for production of both sugar and tobacco as export. Their regent (1637–44) in what they renamed 'New Holland' was a cousin of the

Orange-Nassau line, Johan Maurits of Nassau-Siegen, but he was effectively overthrown by a revolt of Portuguese Catholic planters in northern Brazil in 1645, and the colony was lost entirely in 1649. Capture of the Guyanas and Surinam was secured in 1667 and remained a Dutch possession well into the twentieth century. This later South America plantation life for the Dutch was abetted by further coastal conquests from Portugal that provided the human lifeblood of the commodity production in the form of slaves. In 1637 conquest of the infamous Elmina fortress (originally St George del Mina for the Portuguese) began their control of the Guinea coast of Africa, whence slaves were shipped by the WIC across the Atlantic until the eighteenth century. Despite slave uprisings, including the largest one as late as 1795 on Curaçao, slave trading continued until 1814. Images of black Africans appeared in the Brazilian images of Dutch artists brought over by Johan Maurits: figures by Albert Eckhout (including two full-length 'ethnographic portraits' now in the National Museum, Copenhagen); and Brazilian landscapes with figures working or taking leisure by Frans Post, prepared as both independent pictures for the art market or as decorations for Dutch maps of Brazil.

Indeed, Dutch maps of the entire world, not just of Dutch possessions or European neighbours, became another of their lasting contributions to knowledge during the seventeenth century. Map-making of atlases began in Antwerp in 1570 with the publication of Abraham Ortelius's *Theatre of the World* (*Theatrum orbis terrarum*; widely reprinted until 1612), followed by the *Atlas* of Gerard Mercator, who issued his evergreen world map projection in 1569 and was completing his opus at the time of his death in 1594. Amsterdam enters the picture with Jodocus Hondius, whose firm acquired Mercator's plates in 1604 and updated them until 1637. (Hondius himself died in 1612, and the atlas of the following year includes a two-page frontispiece with portraits of both cartographers.) The ultimate survivor over Mercator-Hondius in the Amsterdam competition for map-making supremacy in Amsterdam was the firm of Willem Blaeu (1572–1638) – and, after his death, of his son Joan (1598–1673). Willem Blaeu made his name starting in 1604 with a four-sheet Mercator projection of the world, but Joan Blaeu was designated in 1638 as the official map-maker to the VOC, so he received updated geographical information from the most recent voyages abroad (including the discoveries around Australia by Dutch explorer Abel Tasman – after whom Tasmania is named – in 1642).

Indeed, the commercial distribution of information that had previously been the exclusive possession of the crown in Portugal or Spain indicates how much printing itself formed part of the commercial nexus of Amsterdam. Dutch outposts in both Brazil and Southeast Asia were proudly displayed, and full-page maps of the continents featured images in the margins of the same kinds of paired exotic figures as Eckhout had made in Brazil for display in the palace of Johan Maurits. Willem Blaeu completed work on his own compendium in 1635, and Joan went on to supplement it with his own *Atlas maior*, which first appeared in 1662 with almost six hundred maps in eleven folio volumes. Hardly a navigational tool, this massive reference work was available only to the wealthy, but it clearly indicated keen Dutch interest in knowledge of the entire globe. Moreover, maps were prized as artworks in their own right, often decorating the walls of Dutch houses and visible in the backgrounds of paintings, including numerous pictures by Vermeer.

That knowledge also appeared in books from Amsterdam publishers, usually ascribed to first-hand knowledge by travellers and often published with illustrations. Most notably, the firm of Jacob van Meurs generated large-scale accounts of distant continents, complete with lavish illustrations and accompanying maps, and in 1664 the States General granted him an exclusive fifteen-year privilege to publish an account of a Dutch embassy to China by Johan Nieuhof. Van Meurs supplemented Nieuhof with illustrated accounts of Japan and America by Arnoldus Montanus as well as a series of books (*Africa; Asia; Syrie*) with seemingly accurate illustrations despite being written by an armchair traveller, Olfert Dapper. The popularity and authority of van Meurs's books is clear from the fact that within a year each of them was snapped up for translation and reprinting with original plates in London by John Ogilby, the Royal Geographer.

But the interest in distant lands had already been percolating for a century, beginning with the book that set de Houtman on his course: *Itinerario*, or 'Voyage or Ship Journey to the East or Portugese India' (Amsterdam: Cornelis Claesz, 1596) by Ian Huygen van Linschoten (1562–1611), who had sailed in 1583 to Portuguese Goa and spent time with the local archbishop, Vicente da Fonseca, before returning to Holland in 1592. Linschoten not only published his observations on fauna and flora as well as people, but included a navigational map actually used for his voyage by de Houtman. In similar fashion, a book about the Ivory Coast of Africa appeared by

Pieter de Marees, *Description and Historical Account of the Gold Kingdom of Guinea* (Amsterdam: Cornelis Claesz, 1602) accompanied by illustrations of local figures in different costumes and professions. Thus besides maps publications with pictures about the exotic wider world were well established in seventeenth-century Amsterdam.

Dutch international commerce and travel also prompted a major breakthrough in international law. Hugo Grotius (1583–1645) was Pensionary of Rotterdam and a close associate of Oldenbarnevelt, so he was imprisoned along with other religious liberals in the Dutch Reformed Church debates. Amazingly, he escaped Holland in his own book chest and spent the rest of his life in exile. His training at the University of Leiden established him as a master of classical languages and a noted religious thinker, placing biblical statements in a historical context. But he became best known to posterity for his legal commentaries. Using historical cases, including the Bible, he argued in 1610 for the republican form of Dutch government under regent oligarchs as promoting liberty and virtue as well as prosperity. In his *De jure belli ac pacis* (On the Law of War and Peace, 1623) Grotius combined political theory with the formulation of international law. But his exile stands as a reminder in Dutch history that toleration remained qualified and anything but universal, especially in the tyranny of religious differences that divided the two conflicting schools of the Dutch Reformed Church.

One outcome of the conservative Synod of Dordrecht by the Reformed Church in 1619, which split the faithful was the decision to commission a new vernacular translation of the Bible, like the recently completed English Authorized

Version (or King James Bible) of 1611. The States General finally agreed to finance the project in 1626, and after nine years the work was completed, published in 1637 as the States Bible (*Statenbijbel*). In twenty years over half a million copies were printed, and like the King James Bible in England the *Statenbijbel* and its commentaries remained authoritative in the Reformed community; like the Luther translation in Germany, the *Statenbijbel*'s phrasing and vocabulary also affected and helped to standardize the Dutch language itself for generations.

REMBRANDT'S FORMATION

Many of these events and intellectual currents affected the man who forms the subject of this book, Rembrandt van Rijn (1606–1669). The city of Leiden, where he was born, played a major role in the early Dutch Revolt. As noted above, Leiden suffered grievously from the 1573–4 siege by Spanish troops but still resisted heroically, so the city came to be revered in Dutch history like Leningrad against the Nazis in the Second World War. To this day, Dutchmen still celebrate Leiden's relief on 3 October, achieved by breaking dikes and flooding the countryside; they annually eat 'freedom fare' on which Leiden citizens survived, traditionally herring and onions, but also modern *hutspot*, a melange of carrots, onions and mashed potatoes. William the Silent gratefully offered the city its new university early in 1575, dedicated to the training of Calvinist preachers, so it quickly became that stronghold of Calvinist orthodoxy and internal debates which so roiled both religion and politics in early seventeenth-century Holland. A massive commemorative tapestry of the relief of Leiden was designed by Joost Lanckert, and Isaac Claesz. van Swanenburg, father of Rembrandt's first master, painted a biblical image of liberation by water, *Pharaoh Drowning in the Red Sea*, for the Leiden Town Hall. Economically, both wool and linen cloth dominated city industry, abetted by major population waves of immigration from the South Netherlands after 1585, which swelled the local population to approximately 45,000, the second largest city in Holland. Isaac van Swanenburg thus also produced a series for the textile guildhall (1594–1612), depicting local drapery production processes.

The outlines of the artist's biography are familiar by now. Though born as the ninth child of ten (sixth to survive) of Herman Gerritsz. van Rijn and Neeltgen Willemsdr van Zoutbrouck, his social standing was definitely middle class, for his father milled malt for beer in Leiden at the city walls near the 'old' Rhine River, and his mother was daughter of a baker. His brothers either followed the family trade or went into artisanal labour: one a shoemaker, another a baker. While his mother's family was Catholic, his father and the family wound up members of the Reformed Church. The artist's first biographical mention appears in 1641 in a *Description of the City of Leiden* by Jan Jansz. Orlers, who claims that Rembrandt went to the Leiden Latin school, linked to the local university, as if he were preparing for a university career or training like Grotius in classical languages for law or theology. His name even appears in the records of Leiden University as enrolled for the study of literature in 1620 – at the very height of religious domination by the conservative theologians at the school. Even as a youth, he would have had to be sensitive to the discredited position of Oldenbarnevelt and Grotius, especially in Leiden.

But Orlers also asserts that Rembrandt's inclination to follow his talent for art compelled his parents to remove him from school and apprentice him for three years to a local painter, Jacob Isaacsz. van Swanenburg, a Catholic, known today from only a few pictures, though his father Isaac Claesz. van Swanenburg was the pre-eminent Leiden painter and designer of stained glass, and his brother Willem was a noted professional engraver. Jacob's principal extant works depict Hell scenes in the old-fashioned but marketable manner of Hieronymus Bosch from over a century earlier, but now transposed into a more learned Latin imagery, such as *The Cumaean Sibyl Showing Aeneas the Underworld*, from Virgil's *Aeneid*. While we cannot draw much inference from Orlers, this unusual school training for a younger son suggests some intellectual promise by young Rembrandt and at least some foundations of learning that he carried into his professional career. Careful attention to ambitious history paintings, especially biblical, ancient or even mythological subjects, with careful attention to their textual sources, would mark his early career and continue throughout. That he considered himself a proud son of Leiden is also evident from the RHL monogram with which he signed some of his earliest paintings ('Rembrandt Harmensz. Leidensis').

To further his career, Rembrandt next spent six months, Orlers tells us, around 1624–5 in Amsterdam, to which he would later move, apprenticed in the studio of Peter Lastman (1583–1633). Lastman, also a Catholic, is far better known today than van Swanenburg, who may have suggested this next stage of training. Lastman enjoyed considerable prestige in the Netherlands for his considerable time spent in Italy (*c.* 1602–7) and even signed his pictures sometimes as 'Pietro Lastman'. His own history pictures depict biblical or classical narratives before architectural ruins based on what he saw in Rome, and his brightly coloured compositions, usually in horizontal format, gather large numbers of full-length figures who interact with quiet gestures while dressed in antique costume, like ancient Roman reliefs. Lastman selects scenes of heightened drama, implying earlier moments coming to a resolution or climax. Rembrandt later adapts several Lastman compositions whenever he selects the same subjects for his work; this return to such a mentor suggests his early ambitions to become a history painter and to master the forms and content of Renaissance painting, as transmitted through the mediation of Peter Lastman.

Rembrandt set up his own studio in 1625 in Leiden and remained there through 1631, even though compared to con-temporary Amsterdam and Haarlem, the city had no major art market. (However, led by Gerrit Dou, Rembrandt's pupil between 1628 and 1631, according to Orlers again, Leiden would soon establish a flourishing new art tradition of *fijn-schilders*, that is, meticulous realist painters of small-scale genre subjects.) Rembrandt was joined in Leiden by a slightly older fellow townsman Jan Lievens (1607–1674), who was recognized early as an artistic prodigy, according to Orlers, and had already studied with Lastman from 1617 until 1619. Possibly these two ambitious young painters figured that they could capture Leiden's nascent art market with the latest visual formulations of Lastman but without guild dues or competition. The two worked closely while Rembrandt remained in Leiden through 1631, prompting assumptions that they even shared a single studio, prohibited by guild regulations in most Dutch cities (Leiden had no painters' guild). Several shared subjects, such as Samson and Delilah and the Raising of Lazarus, clearly prompted a stimulus-and-response series of paintings between the two painters, which suggests a productive friendly rivalry. Like the intimate interaction between Picasso and Braque during the formative years of Cubism, Rembrandt and Lievens were sometimes even confused by their contemporaries as well as by later scholars. Both artists also portrayed each other and utilized some common models or facial types, especially old men and women, in making costumed study heads, known as *tronies* in Dutch studio practice. Such heads became a staple of Rembrandt's early output and across his career, notably including a series of mid-career studies of the face of Jesus.

That Rembrandt and Lievens had attained considerable early reputation is clear from several critical notices. Already in 1628 Rembrandt received a backhanded compliment (in Latin) from Arnoldus Buchelius, an Utrecht jurist, which shows that he had garnered attention even so close to the beginning of his career: 'the son of a Leiden miller is highly, if prematurely, esteemed.' But what really revealed his sudden rise – along with Lievens – is the praise (also in Latin) for both young painters, penned by 1631, before Rembrandt left Leiden for Amsterdam, by the leading taste-maker in the North Netherlands, Constantine Huygens.

Huygens (1596–1687; illus. 36) was the epitome of the learned gentleman-statesman of his day, much like his contemporary English equivalents, such as Samuel Pepys or Thomas Howard, Earl of Arundel. He served as secretary and art agent to stadholder Frederick Henry and remained with the House of Orange until his death. But Huygens also had a literary career, including translation of John Donne into Dutch, and he was an accomplished musician. Thus his autobiography, begun in 1629–31, also includes commentary on the arts and singles out both Rembrandt and Jan Lievens for special mention after he paid a visit to their studio in 1629. Huygens saw them as the youthful vanguard of a new generation of painters, though he continued to regard Rubens as the greatest artist of the Low Countries – a wonder of the world, skilled in all branches of knowledge, and a diplomat as well as a painter adept at any kind of picture. But he predicts that Rembrandt and Lievens will soon surpass their Dutch contemporaries:

> considering a notable pair of youths from Leiden. Were I to say that they were the only ones among all mortals who have equalled what I have formerly described, I would still be greatly underestimating the merits of these men. And were I to say that they would surpass them in a short time, I would not be adding anything to what the best connoisseurs have already predicted for each of them, based on such astounding beginnings. In carefully considering the family of each, no more weighty evidence can I give against the so-called nobility of blood . . . One of my youths, a commoner, has an embroiderer for a father, the other, a miller . . .

He names both Lievens and Rembrandt, in that order, and says that they still appear to be mere boys. Huygens then goes on to compare them, noting that Lievens paints boldly on a large scale 'with audacious subjects and parts', but that he still prefers Rembrandt and relishes his humble Dutch origins:

> I myself venture to state that Rembrandt is superior to Lievens with regard to judgement and in the power to affect feelings . . . wrapping himself up in his work, loves to produce an effect in a small painting and to communicate through abbreviation what you would seek in vain even in the largest paintings by others . . . carrying the highest praises of Greece and Italy to the Dutch, praises for a Dutchman, one who has hardly journeyed beyond the borders of his town.

Huygens goes on to reproach the pair for being self-satisfied and without experience of Italy, which he esteems as magnificent in the achievements of Michelangelo and Raphael. He hopes that their talent will be enriched by that Renaissance experience and 'cause Italians to come to Holland'. Yet he notes their own claim that Italian art has already diffused across the Alps, so that with the 'great demand for paintings from kings and princes north of the Alps, they can see the best Italian paintings outside Italy'. And he grandiloquently compares Rembrandt to the greatest of rival ancient masters, Protogenes, Apelles and Parrhasios, confirming both his ambition and his competitive nature, even towards the noble classical painting tradition. Thus, he claims, these two artists 'in the bloom of youth' want only to prove themselves, so they have no time to waste on distant travel. Huygens ends by praising them for tireless 'diligence and industry', unmatched regardless of occupation or age.

Lievens painted a portrait of a seated Huygens around this time (*c.* 1629). It shows him as a gentleman in elegant costume with lace ruff collar and cuffs but dressed in the fashionable black of the court, accompanied by a gentleman's gloves and beaver hat. He sits in quiet repose, hands in lap, gazing off to the side. His own epigraph to the work from 1632 offers characteristic Renaissance praise for a speaking likeness:

> The speech of this picture is not missing, nor does
>   the voice trip you;
> This is the face of Huygens, who was meditating,
> If you look for the soul, you will each see the one
>   who is full of breath,
> If you will have brought it to Lievens's kind of
>   insight.

Both artists can be documented with important early sales. Lievens, for example, found a primary patron in Orlers himself, who also records astonishment at the range of subjects by one so young: biblical and genre scenes, allegories, still-lifes and a portrait of his mother made when Lievens was only fourteen. Both painters had early works in the English royal collection, probably acquired through intervention by Huygens with English ambassadors in The Hague.

Rembrandt was not the only one who left Leiden in search of greater career opportunity. Probably with an introduction from Huygens, Lievens left in 1632 for London (in Orlers'

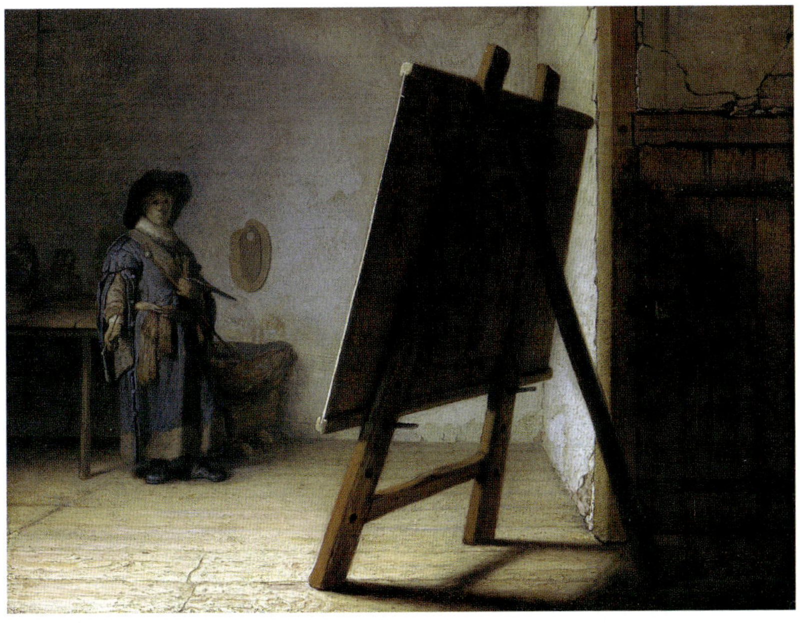

words) to 'see another land and its opportunities'. There he painted portraits of Charles I and members of the royal family, as well as other nobles, but eventually he settled in Antwerp (1635–44), where he married and enjoyed a successful, if less spectacular, career. Basically Lievens reversed the trajectory of Anthony van Dyck, who arrived in England from Antwerp in 1632 and became the favoured court painter. But he finally returned to Amsterdam in 1644, where he participated in two of the most extensive Dutch decorative projects of the century: the 'Orange Salon' (*Oranjezaal*) around mid-century for the court in The Hague and the Town Hall decorations in Amsterdam.

One small early Rembrandt painting (the characteristic noted by Huygens), *The Painter in the Studio* (*c.* 1628; illus. 3),

3 Rembrandt, *The Painter in the Studio, c.* 1628, oil on canvas.

seems to capture both the act of creation and the still-uncertain future – like a large blank canvas – of his career during his Leiden years. Even the room itself is empty and in shabby repair along its doors and walls. By contrast, in most seventeenth-century Dutch paintings of art studios (including several by Gerrit Dou of Leiden), the walls are covered with random, picturesque assemblages of hanging objects or images; other props often rest on tables or floors, items to serve as models: skulls, instruments, swords, globes, and plaster casts or muscle figures (écorchés) for anatomical study of the figure. Yet in Rembrandt's empty space only the large, shadowy silhouette of the easel (with a much larger panel to be painted) occupies the centre. The artist appears in a work smock but also wears a jaunty beret, a signal accessory of Rembrandt in many of his self-portraits. He stands rapt in concentration, ready to advance and use the brush in his right hand, while holding a small palette and additional brushes, plus a maulstick (for resting his hand while in the act of painting). Two extra palettes hang on the otherwise empty wall behind him, and the table behind holds vessels, perhaps with the oils needed as binders for the ground pigments or the varnishes for their surface glazes.

Scholars have observed a resemblance to the face of Rembrandt himself, and this work was also created during the period when Dou was apprenticed in the studio. But the artist depicted can as easily be understood, not as a specific portrait, but rather as generic, conveying the mystery of creation itself out of an artist's own imagination. Since Rembrandt rarely used preparatory compositional drawings or sketches, even on the surfaces of his panels and canvases, before he painted them, this drama of strong lighting, which juxtaposes easel with artist, enacts the very process that he used in making his paintings. This little picture, then, represents bold and conceptual artistic thought, not mimetic working from models, even as it seems to capture the oversized aspirations – self-portrait or not – of the young Rembrandt. Sometime in the year 1631 Rembrandt would move to the big city, leaving Leiden behind for bustling Amsterdam.

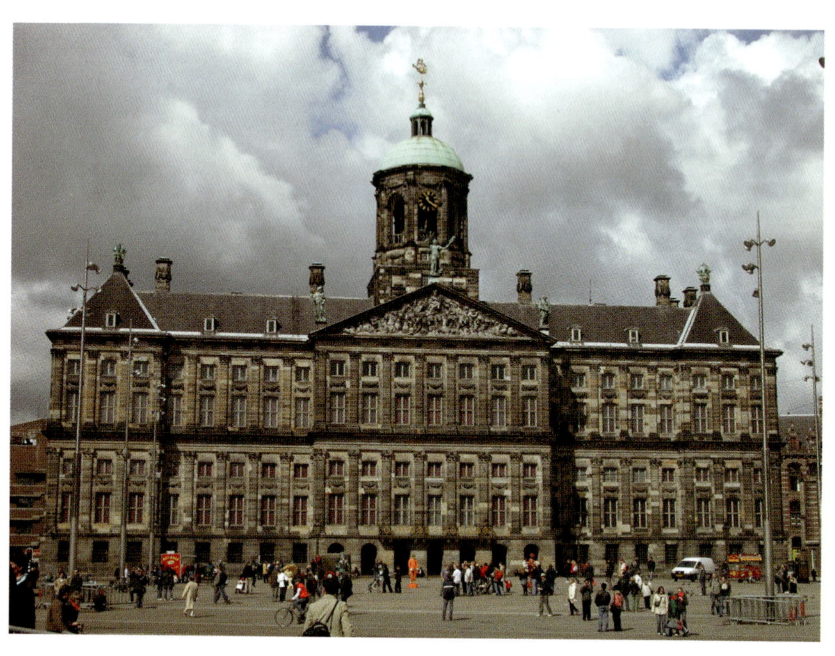

ONE

Representing Amsterdam's Citizens

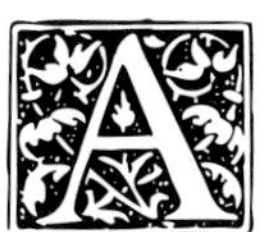

A MSTERDAM WAS ONE OF EUROPE'S fastest-growing cities, expanding from some 30,000 inhabitants in 1570 to about 100,000 in 1620 and as many as 200,000 in 1660. That rapid emergence stemmed from prosperity as the new nexus of world trade, fostered by the two joint-stock trading companies, the VOC (Dutch East India Company; est. 1602) and its New World complement, the WIC (West India Company, est. 1621). The city itself also boldly expanded its urban area in the early seventeenth century (chiefly after 1613; extended from 1656 to 1662) by digging a planned outer belt of canals around its semi-circular southern perimeter, which it gave the lordly names of Emperor's Canal (Keizersgracht), Prince's Canal (Prinsengracht) and the grandest of all, the Gentlemen's Canal (Herengracht). A hundred new bridges and 3,000 new houses adorned the city.

At the centre of this weblike expansion the central organization emerged from the Town Hall (illus. 4) on the main Dam Square, whose construction on the River Amstel gave the town its name. Right after the formal confirmation of national independence for the Dutch Republic with the Peace of Westphalia in 1648, Amsterdam began to build a

4 Jacob van Campen, Amsterdam Town Hall, built 1648–54.

neoclassical palace for the people on the Dam Square to replace an ageing structure, which suffered a terminal fire in mid-1652. Designed by Jacob van Campen, begun in 1648 and continued beyond van Campen's departure in 1654, the massive new City Hall featured a large central citizens' atrium (*Burgerzaal*), whose floor featured an inlaid world map, based on the great atlas publications of Amsterdam by the Blaeu firm.

For the most part, in his relatively infrequent landscape drawings and etchings (26 of them, dated between 1641 and 1652), most of them during the 1640s, Rembrandt chose to record favourite strolls in the nearby countryside and along canals rather than the urban fabric of Amsterdam. The buildings he represented were vestiges of an earlier era, often thatched rural cottages in disrepair in areas of marshland where water and solid ground mix. He exploited the spontaneity of black chalk when he worked from life outdoors, but also produced wide-format panoramas in ink with light wash.

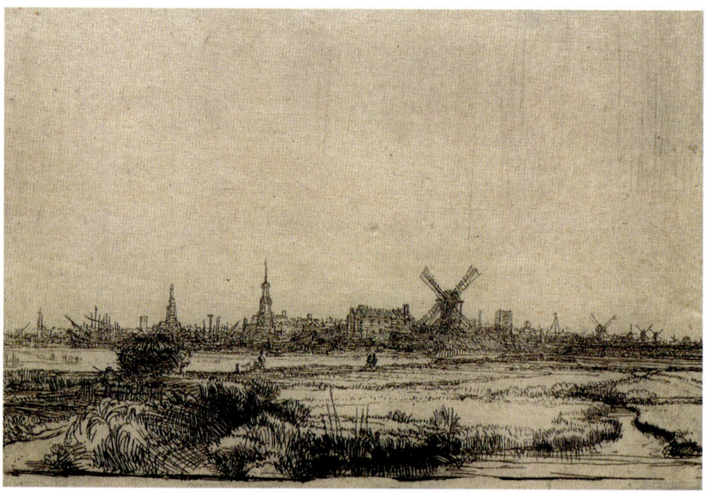

5 Rembrandt, *View of Amsterdam*, c. 1640, etching.

Around 1640 Rembrandt produced his only view of the city of Amsterdam (illus. 5), made from atop a dyke near the large home that he bought in 1639 on Sint Anthoniesbreestraat (St Anthony's Broad Street). Though manipulated for compositional purposes against a high, blank sky, the artist features skyline silhouettes of principal features of Amsterdam: needle-like church towers (most prominently the Oude Kerk, or Old Church); X-shaped windmills on wall fortifications; and masts of sailing ships. In the print's centre warehouses and shipyards of the VOC stand out. The foreground marsh expanse is punctuated by waterways and reeds.

While some painters, notably Gerrit Berckheyde (1638–1698), painted urban scenes of the Dam Square and its imposing new City Hall, Rembrandt made no attempt to represent the heart of his adopted city. Instead, he made images only of the Old Town Hall, a chalk drawing of its demolition and a pen drawing of its ruined condition after the 1652 fire.

As soon as he relocated to Amsterdam, Rembrandt set to work in the most lucrative and promising of painting assignments – portraiture. Already in 1631 he monogrammed ('R[H?] L') and dated one of his largest, most magnificent portraits, painted on the expensive support of mahogany (a West Indies import). This half-length figure, *Nicholas Ruts* (illus. 6), was the first commissioned likeness for Rembrandt, inaugurating one of his most important contributions to art history, chiefly representing his fellow citizens in Amsterdam. In the period from 1631 to 1635 alone, he produced more than forty portraits, which firmly established his career.

Nicholas Ruts (*né* Rutgeerts) exemplifies the life story of many prominent Dutch citizens in Amsterdam. He was a fairly recent immigrant whose Mennonite father, a silk trader, had fled Antwerp to Cologne because of his Protestant beliefs. But by 1617 Nicholas Ruts had arrived in Amsterdam, adopted the Reformed Church and involved himself with Russian trade, a lucrative Dutch exchange of fur imports for finished goods, such as woollens, silks and even church bells.

In Rembrandt's portrait Ruts proclaims not only his personal wealth but its source in the form of his fur hat and the prominent sable trim on his elegant mantle. In a strong side light the sitter stands confidently, turning slightly to direct his steady gaze at the observer. Reserve is suggested by a slightly distancing corner chair, on which his right hand rests; his other hand clasps a sheet of paper, illegible except for another 1631 date, but suggesting a business document. Rembrandt uses delicate brushwork, especially for the textured fur and white lace collar, but he emphasizes Ruts's whiskers through additional scratches on the pigment surface. Face and hands, built of varying colours in layers, animate the warm flesh, while the neutral background around the body is subtly modified to reinforce its dynamic, asymmetrical silhouette. Nor does Rembrandt airbrush the features of Ruts's face; instead, he frankly renders both the wrinkles of his brow and the bags under his eyes. Ruts thus appears to be a figure who is vital, prosperous and serious, but also physically present.

This commission sparked Rembrandt's immediate domination in Amsterdam of the competitive portraiture market, over such earlier rivals as Thomas de Keyser (1596/7–1667;

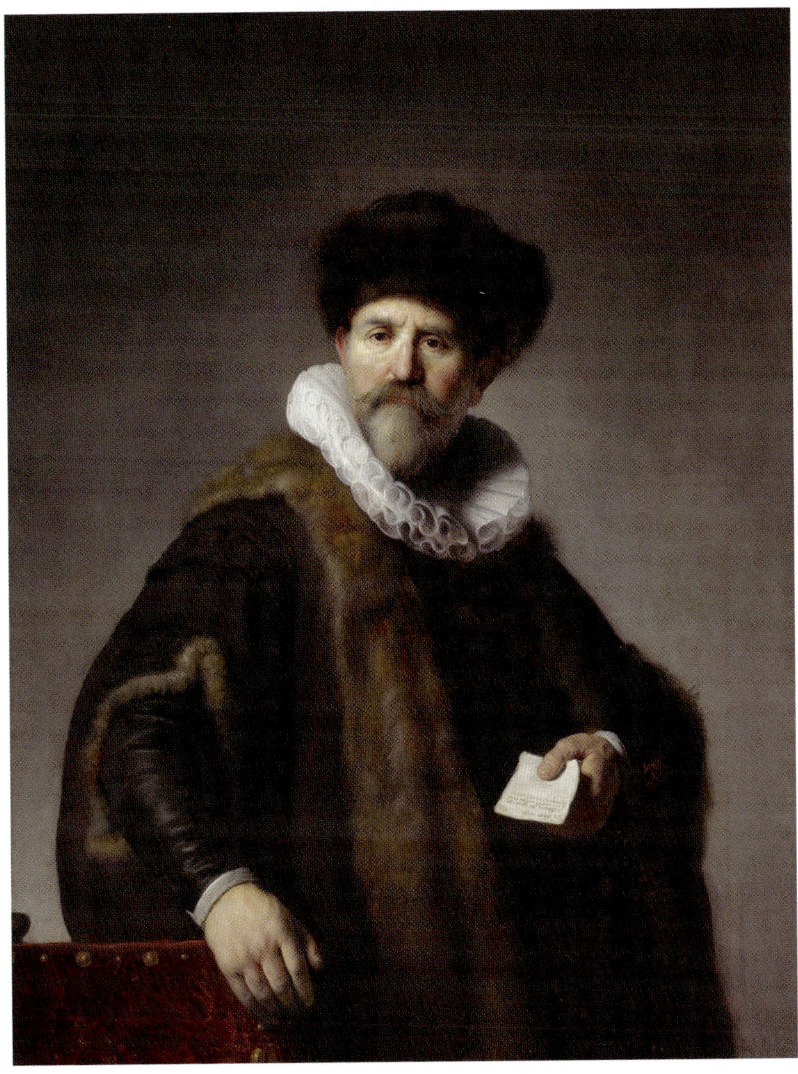

6 Rembrandt, *Nicholas Ruts*, 1631, oil on wood.

see illus. 36; 1627). The commission from Nicholas Ruts probably came from Rembrandt's new Amsterdam affiliation. He was already living with Hendrick Uylenburgh, a prominent art dealer who provided lodging but also studio space for a stable of young painters who fulfilled commissions for him. Uylenburgh, also a Mennonite, provides another telling example of how religious immigration to the commercial centre of Amsterdam could take advantage of a personal network, in this case to match portrait sitters with portraitists, though the dealer might not have had a workshop of his own until he became associated with Rembrandt in 1631. Their close association also had personal implications for Rembrandt, who married Saskia Uylenburgh, the dealer's niece, in 1634 and continued to live with Uylenburgh until 1635. That period marks the most intense output of portraits in Rembrandt's career by far (he made no portraits at all in Leiden); fully half of his hundred portraits were produced while he resided and worked with Uylenburgh.

Like Ruts, one other initial Rembrandt sitter also stems from a Mennonite émigré family of textile merchants from the southern Netherlands: Marten Looten (dated January 1632), who came in 1615 to Amsterdam from Leiden. His commission also probably came to the painter through Uylenburgh, although it is possible that Rembrandt already knew the family in Leiden. The artist ensured identification of his sitter by positioning a legible paper with his name on it in large script along with his RHL monogram.

Throughout his career, most Rembrandt portraits of couples depict husbands and wives as pendant likenesses in separate frames on a modest scale, necessitated by both cost and the scale of rooms in Dutch houses. In those cases, heraldic rules of putting the principal figure on the viewer's left (but also the favourable right-hand side from within the picture) mean that husbands consistently appear in that position, often gesturing towards their wives. Rembrandt seldom got the opportunity to paint larger-scale double portraits (see illus. 8), but when he did he always gave the husband prominence, often in the centre of the composition. In 1633 he painted his first double portrait, a large canvas (but considerably smaller than life-sized) of an unknown, elegantly dressed *Gentleman and Lady in Black* (illus. 7; stolen). This portrait adopts the current Amsterdam fashion of full-length figures in elegant dress, located within enveloping spatial interiors, already popular from Thomas de Keyser. In this work, Rembrandt continues the exquisite detail of many of his Leiden works (a practice long characteristic of his Leiden student Gerard Dou). The husband stands, assertively occupying central space with extended arms, while his wife before him, seated and seemingly distracted in thought, occupies the right front corner, counterbalanced by a chair opposite her. Behind the man a large map – one of Amsterdam's cartographic prizes – decorates the back wall, suggesting the husband's active role in the outside world. An X-ray reveals that a boy once appeared between the couple, surely the object of his mother's gaze; why he was omitted must remain moot. These sitters are not securely identified, but they do match an inventory item for Jan Pietersz Bruyningh, a cloth merchant, and his wife Hillegont Pieterdr. Moutmaker. Certainly their more luxurious dress suggests that they definitely do not belong to the more austere Mennonite sect.

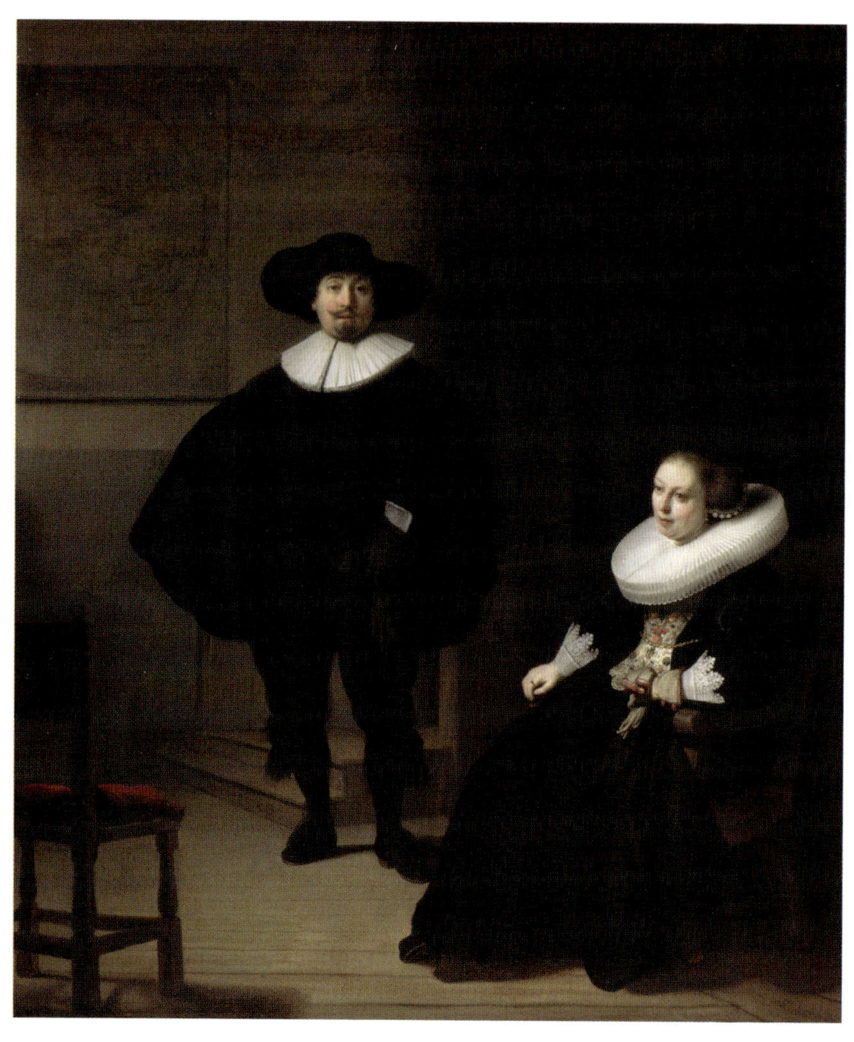

7 Rembrandt, *Gentleman and Lady in Black*, 1633, oil on canvas.

Rembrandt also adopted the same Gardner poses for male and female sitters in other individual early portraits (each paired with a partner in a different pose). He produced another dated (1633) set of pendants, three-quarter lengths, now separated, where the unidentified man has his arms extended and is gesturing towards his wife during the process of rising from his chair, while his wife remains seated with a fan; both sitters face the viewer in dark costumes (with the ever-present lace collars and ruffs) against a dark background. While their white ruffs and collars also light the two Gardner figures as objects of attention, the net result of this double portrait of two individuals evokes a social distance between the couple, albeit still observing gender conventions, including feminine demureness. Rembrandt, however, would utilize the same averted gaze across his career to suggest thoughtfulness or introspection in many figures, especially biblical actors.

A similar-sized pair of early pendant portraits of a couple (*c.* 1633) shows another richly dressed husband and wife, both seated (she rests her shoe on a foot-warmer, a common domestic accessory in cold Dutch interiors). Each is accompanied by a standing child of the same sex who receives coins (the son gets the lion's share), showing continuity of family fortunes. The sitters can be identified: *Jan Pellicorne and Son Casper; Susanna van Collen and Daughter Eva Susanna*. Pellicorne, born in Leiden but resident in Amsterdam, enjoyed a wide commercial network through his wife's family.

Finally, Rembrandt's only extant full-length pair of standing portraits (signed and dated 1634; illus. 8) adopts a showy presentation of court portraits, normally reserved for kings and nobles. It shows instead a wealthy couple, Marten

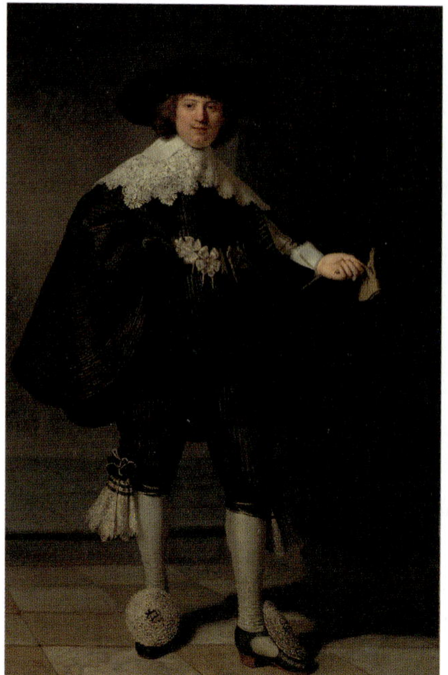
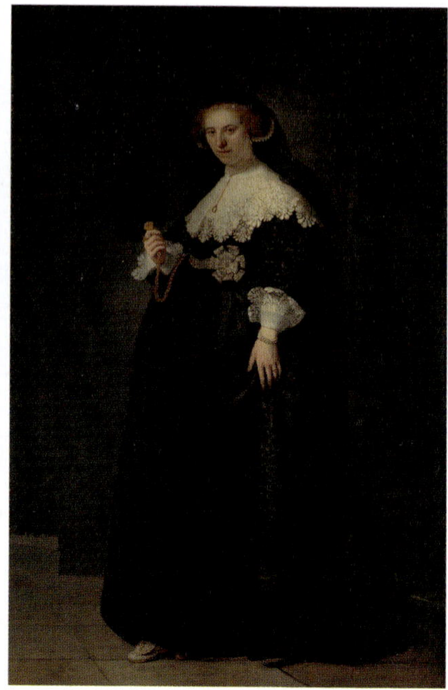

Soolmans and Oopjen Coppit, married the previous year. In this case, the wife's family was an old, established Amsterdam clan; Soolmans stemmed from a prosperous Antwerp family. As usual, the male appears on the favourable viewer left, wearing a broad-brimmed black hat but richly adorned with flamboyant shoes, belt and a fine lace collar, while also casually carrying a kid-leather glove that conveyed aristocratic pretence, even in sober Holland. Her black-on-black satin dress is also complemented with lace at cuffs and neck, plus a pearl choker, and her right hand holds a fan attached to her belt with a gold chain. His left hand with the glove stretches out towards his bride (a marital convention, also used by Frans Hals), even as Soolmans faces forward. Meanwhile, Coppit

8 Rembrandt, *Marten Soolmans and Oopjen Coppit*, 1634, oil on canvas.

turns her entire body to him but still eyes the viewer. A background curtain continues across both portraits. Such a commission from this well-dressed, prominent couple, not to mention their request for full-length pendants, points clearly to Rembrandt's meteoric rise to prominence among Amsterdam's leading portraitists shortly after he arrived in the port city.

AMSTERDAM GROUP PORTRAITS

Young Rembrandt's most ambitious early group portrait in Amsterdam followed soon after his *Nicholas Ruts*. It was commissioned by a physician, Dr Nicholas Pietersz, who adopted the surname Tulp, after the Dutch word for tulip, his favourite flower (also the object of intense desire, 'tulipmania', and commodity speculation in Holland until the bulb investment bubble burst in 1637). Dr Tulp was a surgeon and chief lecturer of the surgeons' guild but also a devout Calvinist; already a member of the Amsterdam town council, he served five times afterwards as city burgomaster. When a new Amsterdam university opened in January 1632, in part as a reaction against the religious orthodoxy of Leiden, it attempted to rival Leiden's famed anatomy theatre (where Tulp had trained), so shortly afterwards Tulp performed a public dissection on a cadaver, obtained from a recently executed criminal, as authorized by city officials. This medical instruction was performed in the upper storey of the repurposed old St Anthony's gatehouse of the city, the Waag, near the Breestraat area where Uylenburgh – and eventually Rembrandt himself – would live.

Rembrandt's commemorative painting of this event (1632; illus. 9) was destined for the boardroom of the Amsterdam surgeons' guild, founded in 1562. The picture builds upon an existing tradition of group portraits of anatomical lecturers, including a work of a group around a central skeleton by Thomas de Keyser for Dr Sebastian Egbertsz (1619). Each participant around Dr Tulp can be identified by name, even the executed criminal, a serial thief (whose alias was 'the Kid', 't Kint).

But Rembrandt's painting is anything but a stiff line-up of heads. Just as he animated some portraits of couples by seeming to arrest their active motion, Rembrandt's asymmetrical composition shows Tulp himself in a momentary pause in his instruction, while his seven auditors all face him. Several figures in an almost pyramidal pile of heads are craning their necks for a closer view of the dissected forearm and hand tendons he is demonstrating. Tulp's are the only hands visible. His knowledge and authority are confirmed by the large open book – probably the lavishly illustrated anatomy by Andreas Vesalius (1543) – placed in the lower right corner, but behind the surgeon as he lectures. Vesalius, in fact, used the same demonstration of finger muscles for his woodcut self-portrait in the treatise.

Some favourite early Rembrandt portrait poses are clearly visible here. The lone forward-facing man at the top of the pyramid of faces anticipates the *Young Woman with a Fan* of the following year, and Tulp himself repeats (but reverses) the same turned pose with a speaking gesture, hand over heart, with even the same distinctive hat from *Martin Looten*. The *Anatomy Lesson* conveys intense concentration through body language by both speaker and listeners, staged as if captured interrupted in mid-sentence and tightly composed rather than loosely distributed. Rembrandt gives balance to the student group but subtly emphasizes some figures over others through variations in position and visibility (the figures at the edges are in profile). He also co-ordinates the lighting of the entire scene to place the brightest spot on the pale cadaver and its loincloth, but he reserves a secondary pool of light for those nearest to the body and for Tulp himself. Meanwhile, Dr Tulp uses his own foreshortened left hand to demonstrate the movement of tendons and muscles under his own right hand with the forceps. (Ironically, the artist seems to have given the awkwardly foreshortened corpse unequally long arms! And technical examination during restoration

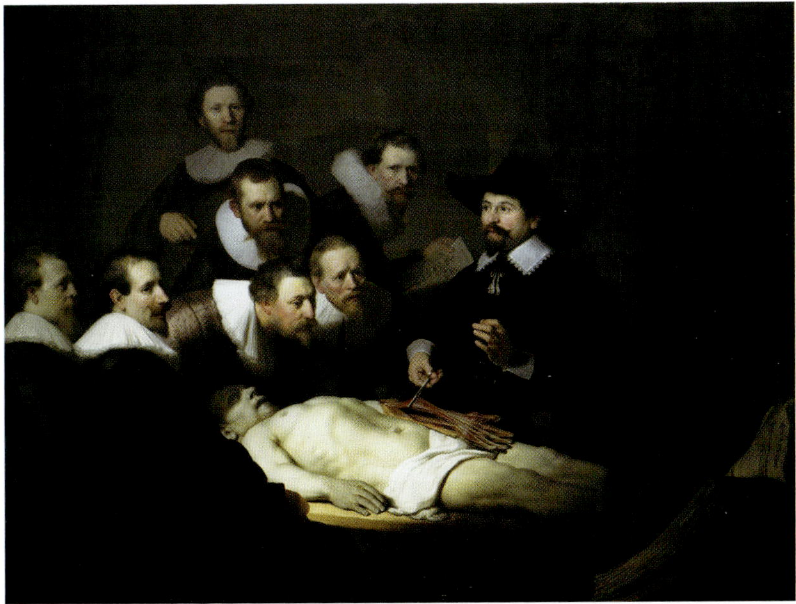

9 Rembrandt, *Anatomy Lesson of Dr Nicholas Tulp*, 1632, oil on canvas.

revealed that originally the convict was painted with only a stump for a right hand, which accounts for the different lengths of his arms as well as the oddly coloured and finely manicured fingers of the added hand on the current paint surface.)

Within a subtle encompassing background niche, all attention is directed to the centre, to the poised medical hand above the cadaver. In effect, although it is a group portrait, Rembrandt has arranged a scene as if it were a dramatic tableau – possibly derived from a Rubens painting, *The Tribute Money* (*c.* 1612), well known from an engraving distributed by the artist. It shows the figure of Jesus boldly making a demonstrative point while facing off the probing faces of his Pharisee antagonists, now transformed into curious student observers.

Group portraits reaffirmed the varied professional and civic communities that defined individuals in seventeenth-century Holland. Dutch citizens participated in craft guilds, served on charitable boards of directors, and drilled in militia companies. Ever since the early sixteenth century either their leaders or the entire group would often commission a large-scale commemorative portrait of that group, whether located at a particular meeting or banquet gathering, or else at a specific event, such as Dr Tulp's anatomy lesson. As with Rembrandt's carefully arranged medical composition, those images are clearly staged, not purely documentary in character. Usually, they were hung at their respective guildhalls, charitable institution boardrooms or militia companies (*doelen*, or target halls, open to the public).

Rembrandt was one of a number of Dutch painters, including one of his own former pupils (Govaert Flinck), who were commissioned to depict the group militias of Amsterdam during the 1630s and 1640s for their enlarged hall, completed in 1627. His large canvas was one of six company portraits commissioned for the same guardroom between 1639 and 1645. This large and encompassing pictorial type was already a century old in Amsterdam, celebrating organizations that dated back to the early fourteenth century. By this time militia companies were commanded by socially prominent citizens who purchased their own arms.

Frans Hals, Rembrandt's older contemporary, produced five separate militia company portraits in his native Haarlem between 1616 and 1639: the St George crossbowmen (three) and the arquebusiers (or musketeers; two) of St Hadrian. (All are housed today in the Frans Hals Museum, itself the Old Men's Almshouse where Hals also painted group portraits of both male and female regents.) Hals even began to paint an Amsterdam militia company in 1633, today nicknamed 'The Meagre Company' (1637; Amsterdam, Rijksmuseum). The convention for these large canvases was to paint the group busily engaged in a meeting, or more typically in Hals's militia gatherings (for example, *Banquet of Officers of the Arquebusiers' Guild*; 1627; illus. 10) gathered at their annual banquet. By the time of Hals and Rembrandt the stalemate of conflicts during the Dutch Revolt meant that a de facto standstill was in effect for their big cities of Haarlem and Amsterdam, so these companies stood on reserve guard with little prospect of active combat except for excursions. Thus their social club elements, especially for the patrician officers of the regent class, emerged more emphatically, so that pictorial compositions subtly emphasize those main group leaders.

Hals's image fairly vibrates with lively brushstrokes in bright colours that offset the sombre black Dutch dress. Diagonal banners and sashes of command distinguish this officer cadre, whose varied poses strike a note of informality and nonchalance. Some gaze out at the viewer while others interact across space. The most important figures remain seated at table; the captain of the company is singled out at near the centre of the picture, not least because of his yellow jacket. Seated and facing the viewer, Captain Michiel de Wael, owner of two breweries in Haarlem, jauntily inverts his drinking-glass to indicate that it is empty. His second-in-command (and brother-in-law) is the colonel, Aernout Druyvesteyn, seated at the far left; most of the interlaced figures, however, still revolve around the command of their captain in the centre.

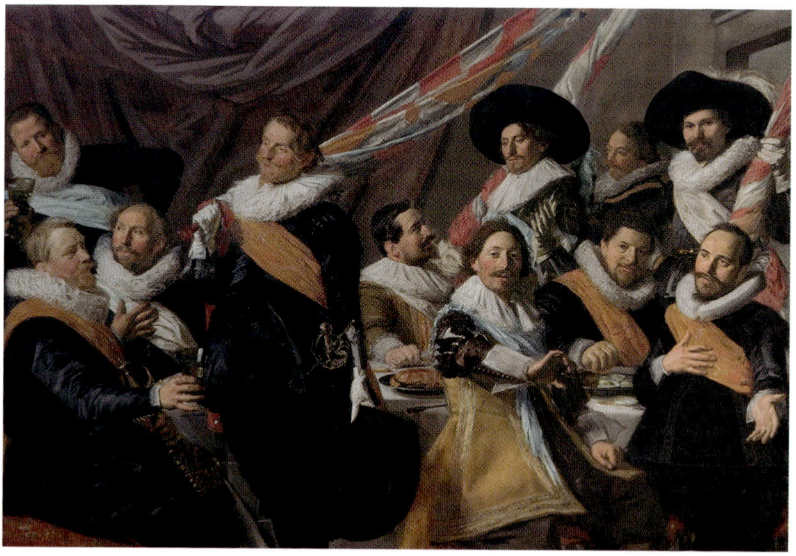

10 Frans Hals, *Banquet of Officers of the Arquebusiers' Guild*, 1627, oil on canvas.

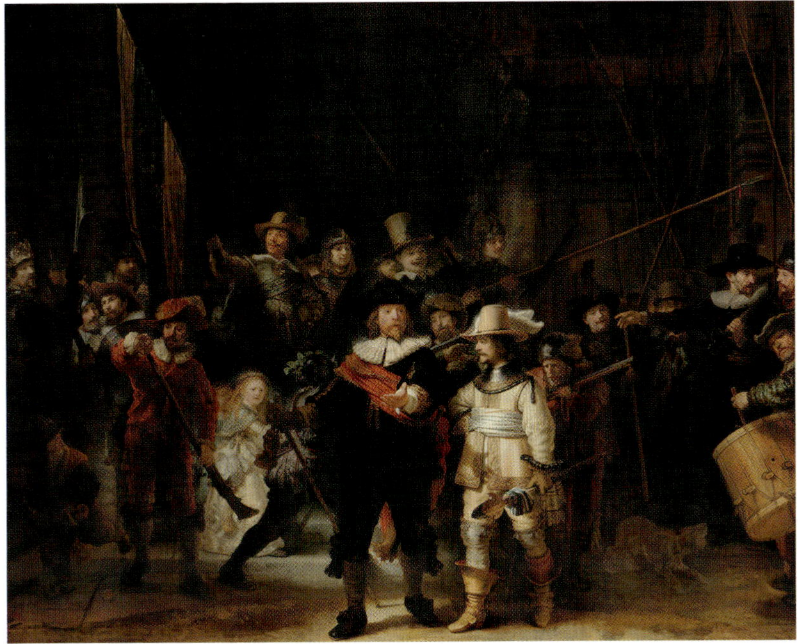

When Rembrandt received his commission from an Amsterdam arquebus company, commanded by Captain Frans Banning Coq and Lieutenant Willem van Ruytenburgh, completed in 1642 (illus. 11), he sought to avoid the appearance of either a motionless choir-like row of standing figures (as in Thomas de Keyser's 1632 guardsmen group portrait, with its leaders larger and central) or else indulging at a festive banquet. Instead, he animated the group as if it were about to mobilize for drill with banners and weapons at the ready. This famous large canvas has come to be known as the *Nightwatch*, in part due to its darkened surface over time, now restored, but also because such militia companies went on night patrols in their later history. The original, now cut down

11 Rembrandt, *'The Nightwatch'*, or *Militia Company of Captain Frans Banning Cocq*, 1642, oil on canvas.

to fit a smaller space in the city hall after its original site in the militia guildhall, was copied in its original format, revealing that it was once larger at the left and across the foreground and contained a larger crowd of 34 figures.

Carefully constructed though seemingly spontaneous, Rembrandt's *Nightwatch* still gives prominence to its leaders. Banning Cocq in particular stands front and centre, wearing a bright red sash of leadership while seeming about to emerge from the picture space; under bright illumination his outstretched, foreshortened arm gestures in command and even casts a shadow on his second-in-command. Banning Cocq married into an Amsterdam patrician family and followed his father-in-law to serve in several city offices, including later roles as alderman and burgomaster. Receiving the order to march out, the lieutenant stands deferentially beside him; dressed in a brilliant yellow uniform with strong three-dimensional embroidery, he carries a ceremonial weapon, a halberd.

Behind these two principals the hierarchy continues, where the sergeants flank the company at the sides. Across the painting the militia now gathers; many of them load or shoulder their muskets, the weapons that identify their group. Others carry lances and an ensign proudly shoulders the company banner as if going to battle. Their collective assembly suggests that the group is busy marshalling for an actual event, and some scholars have tried to see a specific occasion represented in the image, such as the recent ceremonial entry into Amsterdam by exiled queen mother Marie de' Medici of France (1638), where large triumphal arches in the city streets resembled the one at the rear of the picture. This musket drill – loading, firing and clearing the firing-pan

— actually reprises several instructional illustrations from a Dutch army manual of firearms, engraved by Jacques de Gheyn II (1607). In addition, the powder boy, wearing a comically oversized helmet at lower left, brings ammunition to the troops, while the drum and banner carriers rally a corps on the march or in the field. The suggestion of antique armour or helmets hearkens back to a more glorious era of civil military defence from the early Dutch Revolt of the previous century.

Rembrandt also inserts an incongruous little girl behind Banning Cocq; she appears in bright light and wears a golden dress that complements the lieutenant's uniform, while moving against the direction of the march. Crowned with a golden band, she hangs a chicken at her belt, whose prominent claw (a griffin claw; shades of Harry Potter) served as a symbol of the company, and she wears a drinking-horn of the kind used at company banquets. Thus with these emblems of the militia upon her, she appears like an allegory or mascot of the group and further undercuts the suggestion that this composition represents an actual company event.

While some scholars interpret the picture as having an unequivocal celebratory character in praise of the company, recently others (Schama, 1999; Carroll, 2002; Berger, 2007) have observed an ironic disunity in the entropy of their momentarily chaotic assembly, which would contrast with the orderly rows and earlier unified heroism of the Dutch Revolt. Clearly Rembrandt still honoured the other sixteen subscribers to this group portrait by showing them massing for action. But he may also have represented their civic character, like most other militia company group portraits, as only ceremonial or at most defensive in character, and thus unsuited to the militaristic goals of the stadholder and his war party in The Hague.

AMSTERDAM PATRICIANS AND OTHERS

With the Banning Cocq militia company we see Rembrandt making inroads with the regent class of his adopted city, for he used the full-length presentation of court portraiture for the pendants of Marten Soolmans and Oopjen Coppit, who were also early collectors of his work. Another imposing full-length male portrait (1639; illus. 12) shows its patron to have held overt aristocratic pretensions. A glove lies casually at his feet as he stands nonchalantly, resting his right arm before an enormous doorway with steps, another sign of conspicuous consumption in crowded Amsterdam. While still dressed in sober and respectable Dutch black, his clothing is tailored in sumptuous fabric. Documents reveal that Rembrandt painted a large, expensive portrait for one of the members of the city's most politically powerful families, Andries de Graeff, who was only 28 years old in 1639 but would go on to succeed his brother Cornelis de Graeff as burgomaster two decades later. Moreover, Andries initially rejected the painting made by Rembrandt, even though he eventually paid the high 500-guilder fee after a lawsuit by the artist. Perhaps that conflict with the artist might account for the glove on the ground, a traditional challenge to a duel. Although Rembrandt continued to paint portraits, he never succeeded after the *Nightwatch* in making inroads with the closed patriciate of Amsterdam – with one major exception: Jan Six (1618–1700).

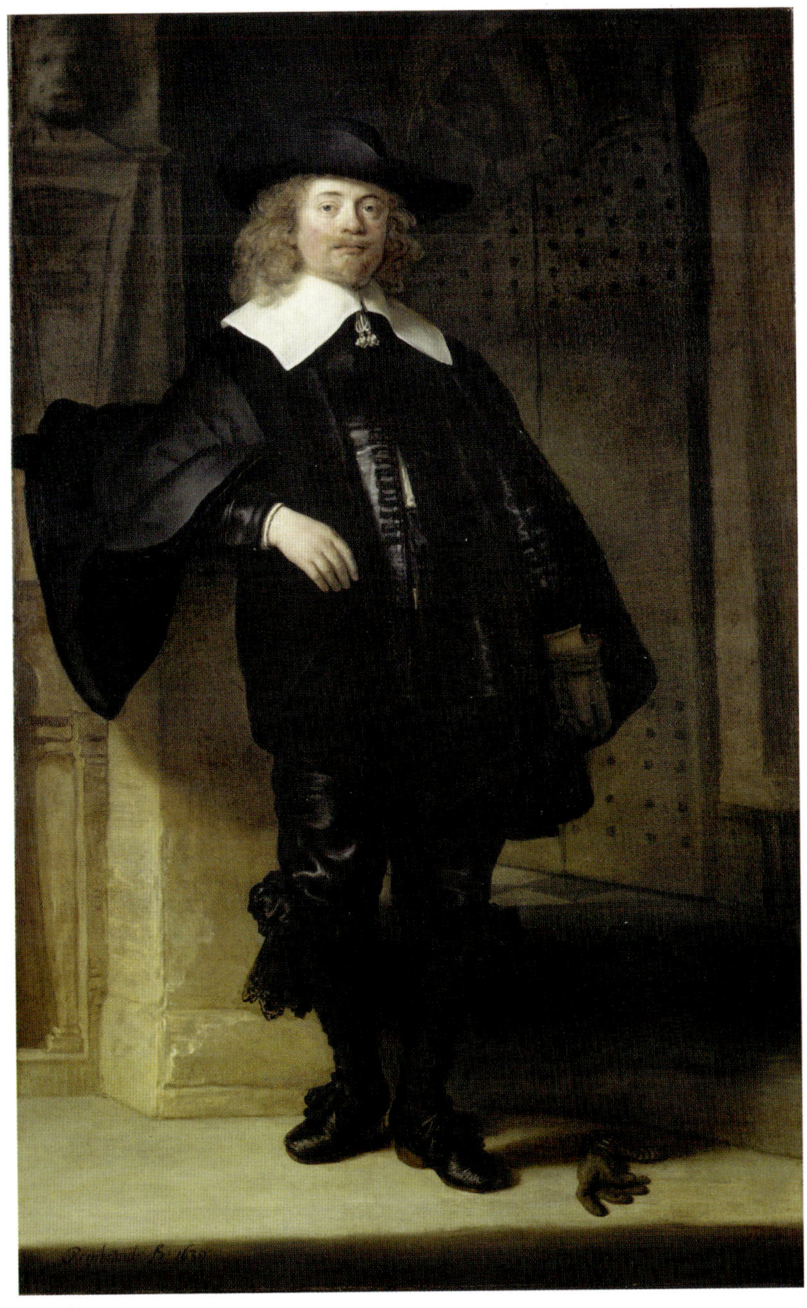

12 Rembrandt, *Man Standing in Doorway (Andries de Graeff?)*, 1639, oil on canvas.

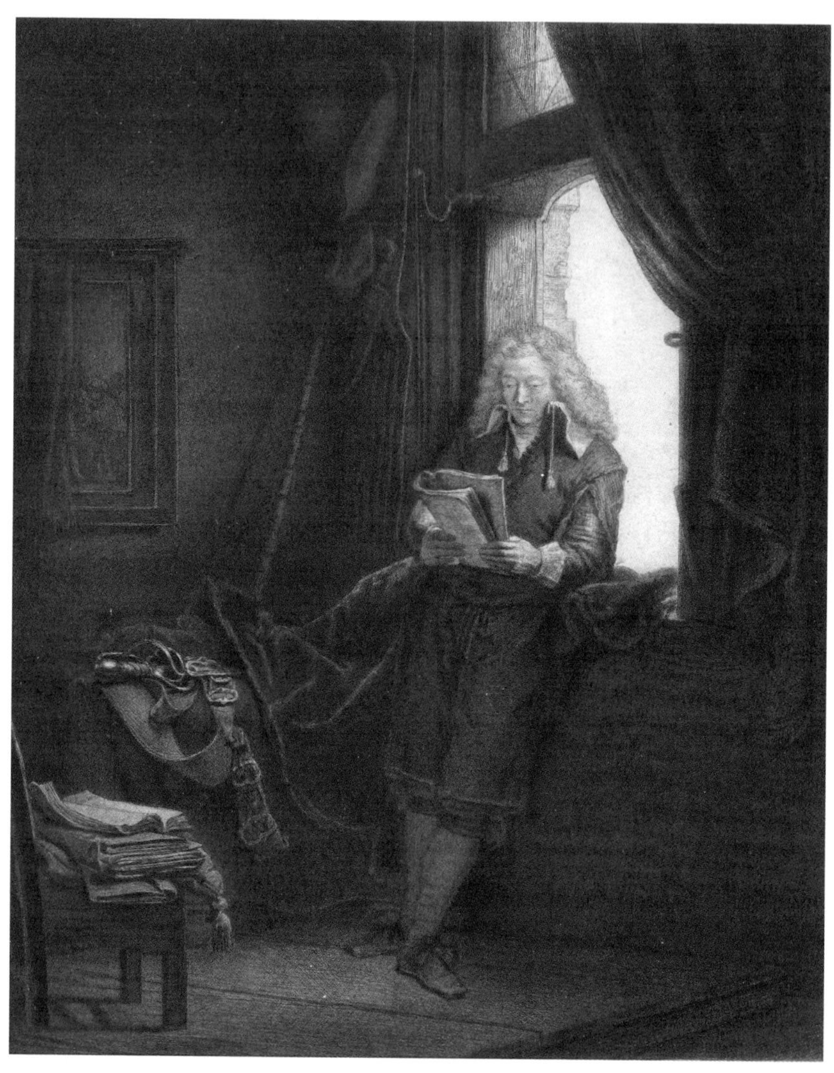

13 Rembrandt, *Jan Six*, 1647, etching.

Jan Six came from a family of Huguenots, French Protestant émigrés, who came to Amsterdam in the late sixteenth century and prospered as cloth merchants and silk dyers. Six prided himself on his Latin poetry and his devotion to the arts. He published several plays, including a verse drama of the tragic Medea myth, for which Rembrandt produced an etched frontispiece illustration, *The Marriage of Jason and Creusa*, in 1648. Six married Dr Tulp's daughter in 1655, so his stature in the city was secure; he became burgomaster later, in 1691. Six also loaned Rembrandt money several times.

Rembrandt's first likeness of Six is also full-length and aristocratic; it is not a painting but an etching, dated 1647 (illus. 13). It records a gentleman of leisure, relaxing in his spacious canal house on the Amstel (open for visits). Rembrandt made three preparatory drawings (still in the Six House) for someone who must have been a major patron to him. Once more a standing sitter in fashionable attire is shown relaxing, leaning casually against a bright windowsill while absorbed fully in his reading, his collar loosened in informal intimacy. To indicate his love of arts and learning, a framed artwork hangs nearby, dimly visible on the adjacent wall, near a pile of book volumes. A discarded aristocratic sword, possibly worn with a militia company (where Six was an officer), occupies a surface. In the shadowy interior inky black shadows show Rembrandt's consummate command of the etching medium. Rembrandt also painted a half-length portrait of Jan Six in 1654 (still in the Six House), rendering his face with subtle detail but using bold brushwork (like Frans Hals) for the red cloak, lace cuffs and the glove that he is adding while departing his private quarters. The artist also contributed two pen drawings to Six's 'friends' album' (*album amicorum*), choosing classical subjects, notably *Homer Reciting Verses* (see illus. 51; 1652).

Rembrandt, however, made numerous portrait etchings in the late 1640s of non-patrician citizens, including an etched *Self-portrait* (1648; see illus. 55). Among these works is his only etching of a fellow-artist, *Jan Asselijn* (c. 1647–8; illus. 14). Asselijn (c. 1615–1652), a landscape specialist, had recently returned from travels in both Italy and France, and he is known as one of the innovators in what is now called the 'Italianate landscape' genre of Dutch painting. Ironically, Rembrandt's own most productive period of landscape drawings and etchings, inaugurated with his small view of Amsterdam (see illus. 5), featured a much more documentary character of his local walks near the city, often rendered with high skies on a horizontal format. Asselijn, by contrast, constructed exotic foreign settings that featured ancient ruins or Roman hillsides under glowing sunset skies or imaginary Mediterranean ports.

Anthony van Dyck notably produced a large group of over a hundred portrait prints that featured many of his fellow Antwerp artists and patrons; first issued in 1645 in Antwerp, that series might have sparked Rembrandt's own unusual turn to depict in his work Asselijn or else evoked a commission for the print by the ambitious sitter or alternatively by his brother Thomas, a textile merchant documented in later Rembrandt transactions.

Before an easel with one of his paintings of ruins in progress, the painter poses in elegant formal costume, including a broad-brimmed top hat. Both palette and brushes as well as books on an adjacent table-top suggest that he is a

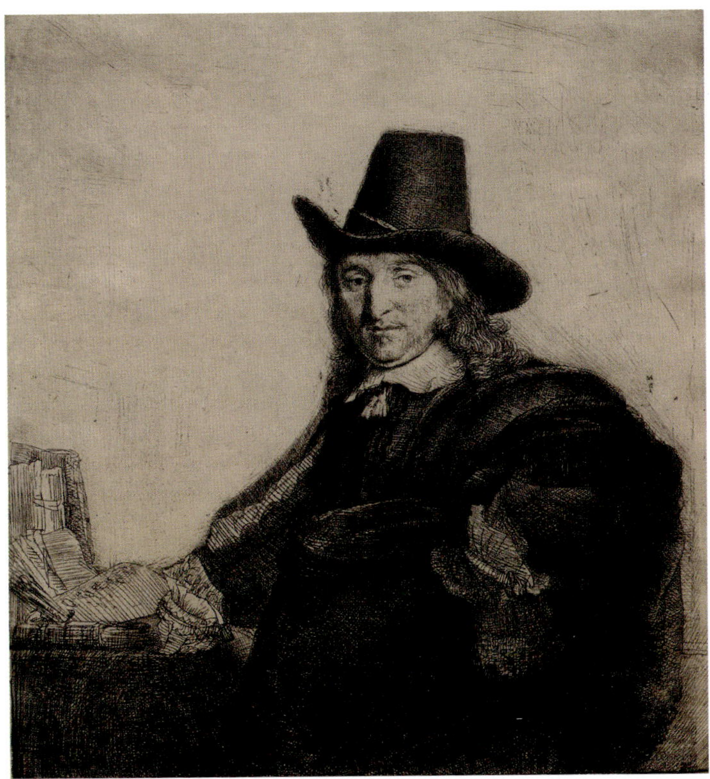

learned artist, while his stance conveys confidence through his assertively foreshortened, bent 'Renaissance elbow'. It also serves to obscure the deformed left hand of the painter, who was known in Rome by the Dutch artistic community (*Bentveughels*, or 'birds of a feather') by the nickname 'the little crab' (*Krabbetje*). His gentility is emphasized further in a second state of the print, when Rembrandt removed the background easel but still left the palette and books.

Another unusual commissioned portrait print (1647; illus. 15) by Rembrandt at this moment is his likeness of Jewish

14 Rembrandt, *Jan Asselijn*, c. 1647–8, etching.

physician and poet Ephraim Bueno (1599–1665), who lived on the same city block but was born in Portugal. His father, also a doctor, was called to the deathbed of stadholder Maurits in 1625. Rembrandt based this print on a prior, more informal half-length oil sketch (Amsterdam, Rijksmuseum); both Van Dyck and Frans Hals also used preliminary oil sketches for their portrait prints, usually reversed in the printing process. Rembrandt shows Bueno pausing with his hand on a staircase banister, poised to depart, as in the later Six painting. He too wears contemporary Dutch dark formal dress and hat. Jan Lievens also etched a seated portrait of Bueno (undated, but after 1644, when Lievens returned to Amsterdam). It bears a more elaborate Latin inscription that compares him to an earlier 'Medicus Hebraeus', Avenzoar (Ibn Zuhr), a famous twelfth-century Andalusian doctor from the same region as Bueno's ancestral family.

Rembrandt never abandoned portrait painting, which became all the more important as an income source for him later in life after his 1656 bankruptcy and his resulting straitened circumstances. One remarkable and enormous commission of this final period was a full-length, life-sized equestrian portrait (1663?) of both horse and rider, painted for a prominent banker, Frederik Rihel (1621–1681). In that picture the sophisticated rider practises the levade, a move where the horse raises both front legs, popularized in court circles as part of their equestrian dressage exercises, thus appropriate for depicting royal commanders in the field. The image commemorates the sitter's proud participation in a prestigious 1660 event of a ruler entry into Amsterdam, which honoured Mary Stuart, sister of Charles II of England, widow of the late

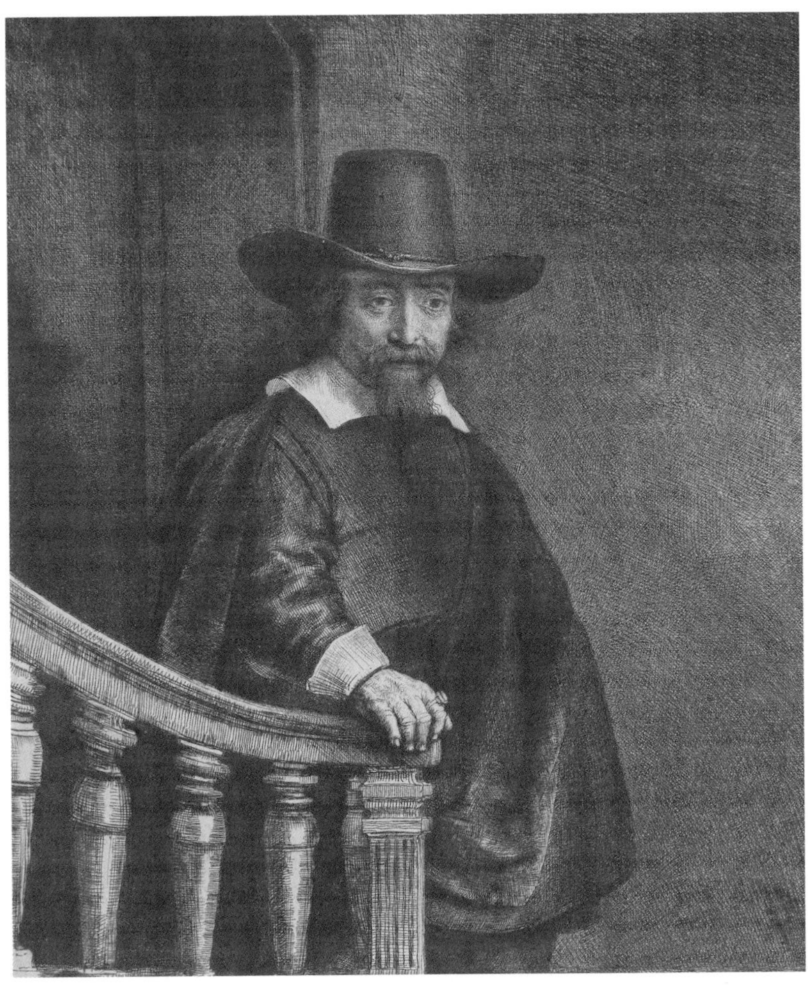

stadholder William II and mother of William III, who would attain the throne of England after 1688 as co-regent William with his cousin Mary.

But Rembrandt's most important sitter in his final decade was the fabulously wealthy Jacob Trip (1575–1661), painted

15 Rembrandt, *Ephraim Bueno*, 1647, etching.

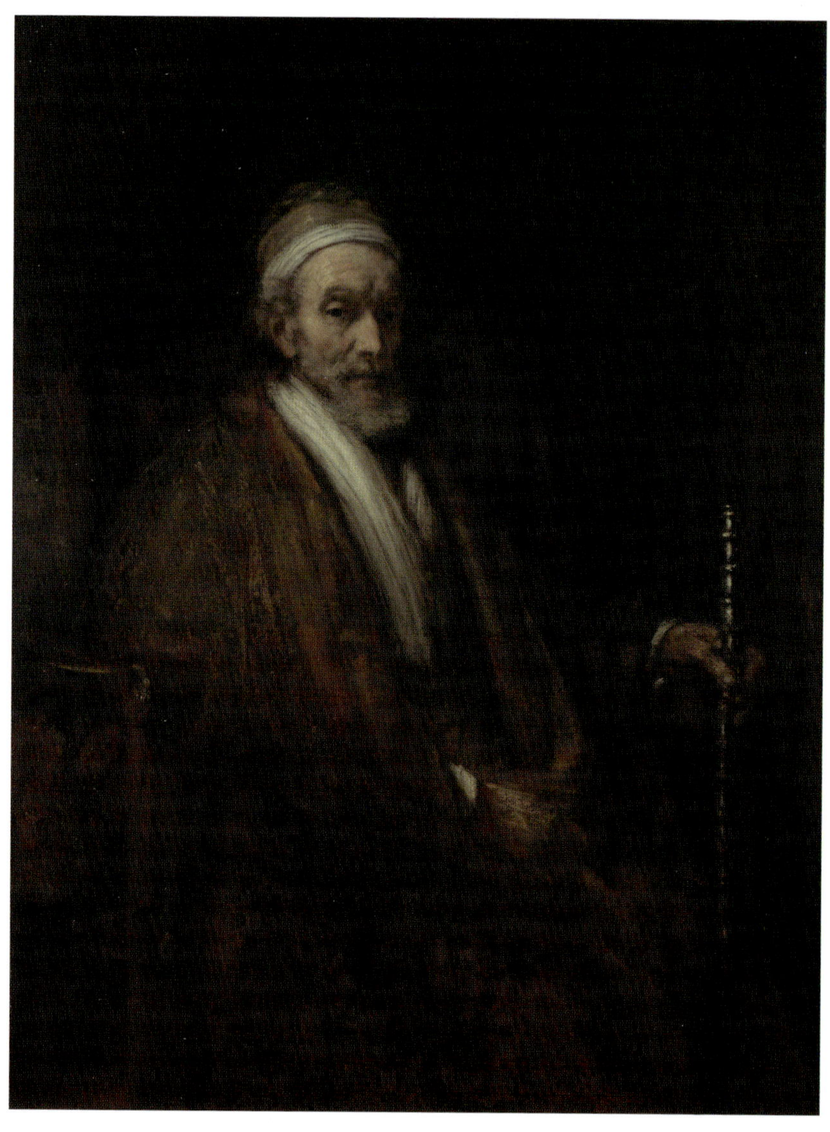

16 Rembrandt, *Jacob Trip*, c. 1661, oil on canvas.

near the end of his life in oblique lordly majesty from his armchair (*c.* 1661; illus. 16) and paired with a pendant portrait of his wife Marguerite de Geer. Trip's family had just built the grandest (that is, widest and tallest) home in the most up-to-date, classicizing style (designed by leading architect Justus Vingboons, between 1660 and 1662), complete with pediment, pilasters and garlands, located on one of the most prestigious canal sites in Amsterdam, the Kloveniersburgwal, near the militia company home. (Today it is home to the Dutch Academy of Arts and Sciences.) Originally shippers, the Trips built up an industrial base of iron mining and arms dealing, particularly through their monopoly based in Sweden (painted panels with Swedish waterfalls and mountains adorn the Trip House). But they were relative newcomers to Amsterdam, and were not included in the regent class.

Rembrandt's pupil from Dordrecht, Nicolaes Maes, painted portraits of the Trips before he did. This portrait of Jacob is broadly brushed with reduced colour, like other works in the manner of Rembrandt's late painting style, extending the experimentation in his Six painting. This bold painting technique for its wealthy sitter can be compared across three decades to the early meticulous textures for *Nicholas Ruts*. But here the commanding posture of Jacob Trip, reinforced by his cane, held like a sceptre, asserts even grander, family-based consciousness of power. A subtly lower point of view below his chair arm elevates the sitter to a position of superiority; his stern look turns towards the viewer but moves away from the oblique axis of his body, as if to show further condescension. This kind of presentation of rank stems from group portrait compositions, such as the militia companies by Hals. He wears the *tabaard*, a robe associated with learning and usually worn by scholars or clergymen.

In contrast, Marguerite de Geer, an equally assertive spouse from a powerful marital alliance, sits fully forward, wearing an old-fashioned thick lace collar and cuffs while she faces the viewer directly with a stare, completely without the usual wifely deference to her husband or oblique modesty before the viewer. Perhaps her visual independence indicates that her husband had already died when her own portrait, more finely fashioned, was completed. In any case, she is portrayed as a ruling family matriarch.

Around the time of the *Trip–De Geer* portraits, Rembrandt completed one last group portrait in his latter years: the 'Syndics', or sampling officials (*Staalmeesters*), of the Amsterdam Drapers' Guild (1662; illus. 17). This elite merchant group, appointed by the city burgomasters, provided quality control for processed and dyed local cloth products. Their group portrait, slightly larger than life-sized, would have hung above the mantel in the guildhall across the canal from the militia guilds (*doelen*). Once more Rembrandt animates his group into a dynamic unity rather than a row of heads, establishing a hierarchy of rank while according each individual promin-ence and dignity with balanced lighting, much in the manner of Hals's militia banquets (but in sharp contrast to the *Nightwatch* group). As usual with group portraits, all of them can be identified by name. Here all the sitters, still dressed in sober Dutch black with hats, seem to acknowledge the viewer with responsive outward and downward glances. As in *Jacob Trip*, Rembrandt uses a lowered point of view, adapted to the higher mantel location. Visual attention begins at the corner of the table, where the carpet table-covering is brightest; above that spot the leader of the group, the chairman, who sits with a ledger and extends his foreshortened right hand commandingly like Frans Banning Cocq. All other figures frame him and turn towards him, including the figure half-standing on his right side; behind him the bareheaded shop steward stands quietly. Rembrandt prepared this painting with special care: three figure drawings survive, and X-rays reveal numerous subtle changes of position. Perhaps no other Amsterdam group portrait so vividly conveys the bourgeois civic virtues of probity and seriousness of these solemn judges of Dutch business activity.

Around the time of the 1648 Peace of Westphalia in Münster, which confirmed the independence of the United Netherlands and its seven provinces as a nation, Amsterdam

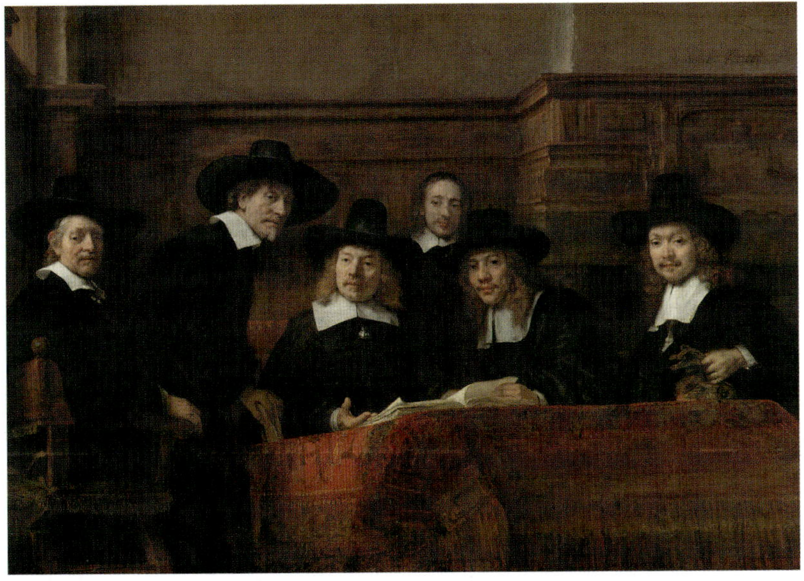

17 Rembrandt, *Syndics of the Drapers' Guild*, 1662, oil on canvas.

celebrated the imminent cessation of combat from the Dutch Revolt by building a worthy palace for the people on the main Dam Square. That enormous and magnificent structure was designed with classical vocabulary of a triangular central pediment and attached pilasters, plus a central cupola, by Jacob van Campen (dedicated in 1655; see illus. 14; now a royal palace). The building was open to all, centred around a core space, the Burgerzaal (Citizen's Hall), that was paved with a world map in two hemispheres (based on the Blaeu atlas, published in Amsterdam) to show the city's global trade reach. It towered at 25 m tall and had a floor plan 34 m square. Sculpted pediment reliefs by Artus Quellinus paid tribute to the city. The front pediment, facing the main Dam Square, depicted sea gods paying homage to a female allegory of Amsterdam. Under a huge bronze figure of Atlas carrying the world on his shoulders atop the rear facade, the other relief by Quellinus shows the Four Continents like the three magi, bringing their bounty as tribute to the central personification of the city.

To decorate the City Hall, Amsterdam chose both mythological and biblical subjects as well as ancient Roman histories, especially of the heroic Dutch ancestors, the Batavians, in their revolt against the empire, reported by Tacitus. All were deemed suitable inspiration for the city's officials, whose offices surrounded the central space. For these painted decorations, commissioned beginning in 1655, Rembrandt himself was neglected in favour of two distinguished former students from the 1630s: Govert Flinck and Ferdinand Bol. Flinck in particular received the commission to decorate the four high arches of the corridor around the gallery perimeter of the building's upper storey. He was well connected with the powerful De Graeff ruling faction, including Andries and his burgomaster brother Cornelis, but Flinck's sudden death in 1660 opened up new opportunities for other artists. Jan Lievens, Jacob Jordaens of Antwerp and other artists were recalled to fill the void, and even Rembrandt eventually also had his chance to participate.

Characteristic of the original plans for paintings on the interior are large mantelpiece canvases by both Flinck and Bol. For the council chamber Flinck produced a canvas of the kneeling *Solomon's Prayer for Wisdom* (1658; 1 Kings 3:9), painted to inspire city regents to seek divine counsel for their decisions. For the burgomaster's room Flinck had already painted a canvas about a Roman consul based on Plutarch, *The Incorruptible Marcus Curtius Dentatus* (1656), who maintains his integrity despite the blandishments of the rival Samnites and prefers turnips to gold. Also for that same chamber Bol competitively offered his *Pyrrhus and Fabritius* (1656), another Plutarch tale where even an elephant fails to frighten or intimidate Fabritius, despite the efforts of his enemy, King Pyrrhus.

The seventeenth-century Dutch also readily identified with the ancient Hebrews because of divine protection in their struggle to liberate themselves from bondage to a cruel ruler – Pharaoh in Egypt. Thus when Bol painted a canvas for the Aldermen's Chamber (Schepenkamer), he selected *Moses with the Tablets of the Law* (1659; illus. 18). Bathed in light, the patriarch descends from Mount Sinai with the decalogue and stands apart from the wondering people below, who gesture boldly in their brightly coloured, exotic costumes. This composition may derive from Rubens's formulations of the

Assumption of the Virgin, replicated in prints, where the Virgin hovers above gesticulating apostles.

When Jan Lievens was enlisted to participate in completing the arched lunettes of the gallery, his topic was an obscure moment from the cycle of the ancient Batavian revolt under Claudius Civilis against the Romans (69 CE), as recorded by Tacitus in Book Four of the *Histories*: *Brinio Raised on a Shield* (1661; sketch on paper) shows the election of an allied leader.

Rembrandt also adopted the Claudius Civilis story. His large painting, the *Oath of Claudius Civilis* (1661–2; illus. 19), represents a nocturnal oath of conspiracy that began the revolt. But it survives only in a long narrow fragment, whose original, towering interior space, rather than a sacred grove, appears in a compositional sketch (1661), only to be drastically cut down. Flinck's surviving sketch (1659) called for a table seen from the side with the hardy hero, naked from the waist up and in profile, receiving homage from an armoured supplicant, perhaps a Roman defector, and clasping his hand. Rembrandt instead offered a composition akin to the *Syndics of the Drapers' Guild* and ultimately keyed to the banquet character of the event. His looming figure of a crowned Civilis sits left of centre, surrounded on both sides by facing conspirators, barbarians all seen from below (emphasized further by steps in the original setting) under the eerie glow of a hidden lamp that colours the table surface – a lighting effect that goes back to the artist's earliest experiments. But Rembrandt also emphasized here the wider range of figure types – bearded and unbearded, young and old, elegant and common – who touch swords in the central

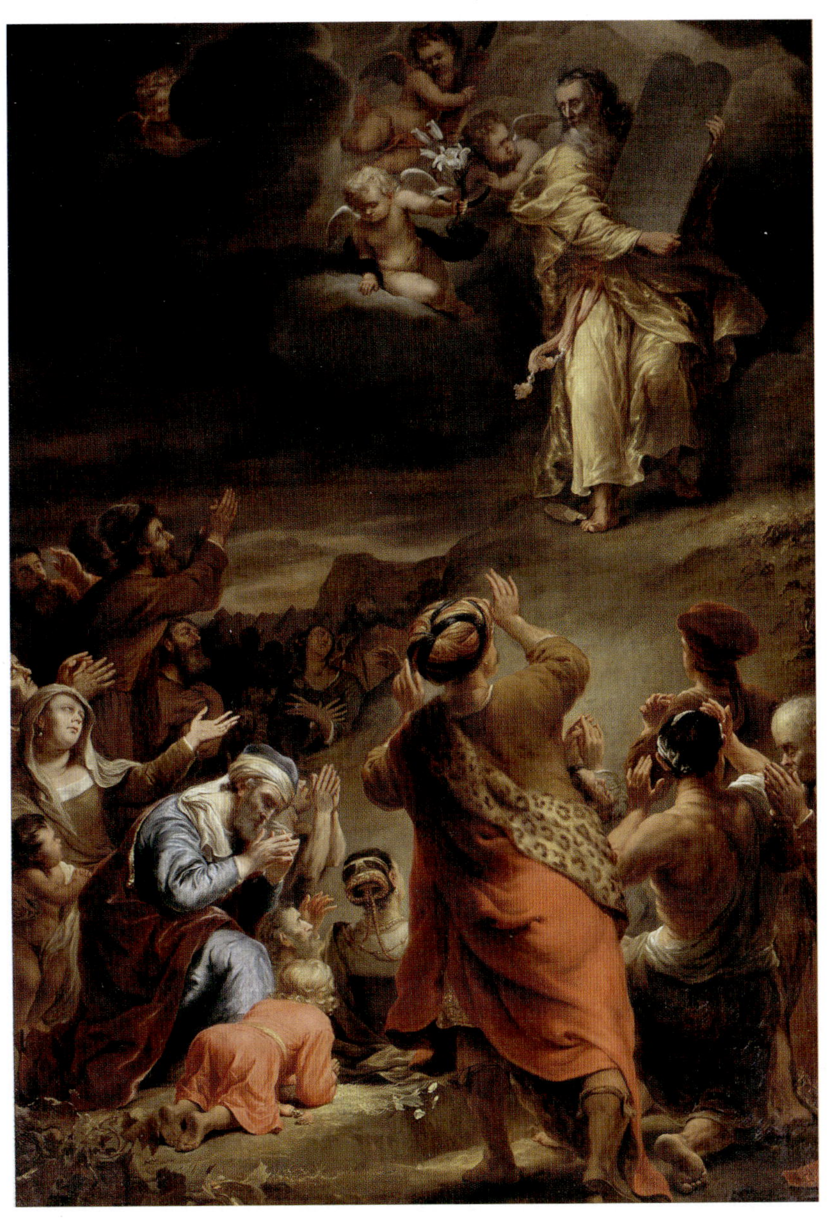

18 Ferdinand Bol, *Moses with the Tablets of the Law*, 1659, oil on canvas.

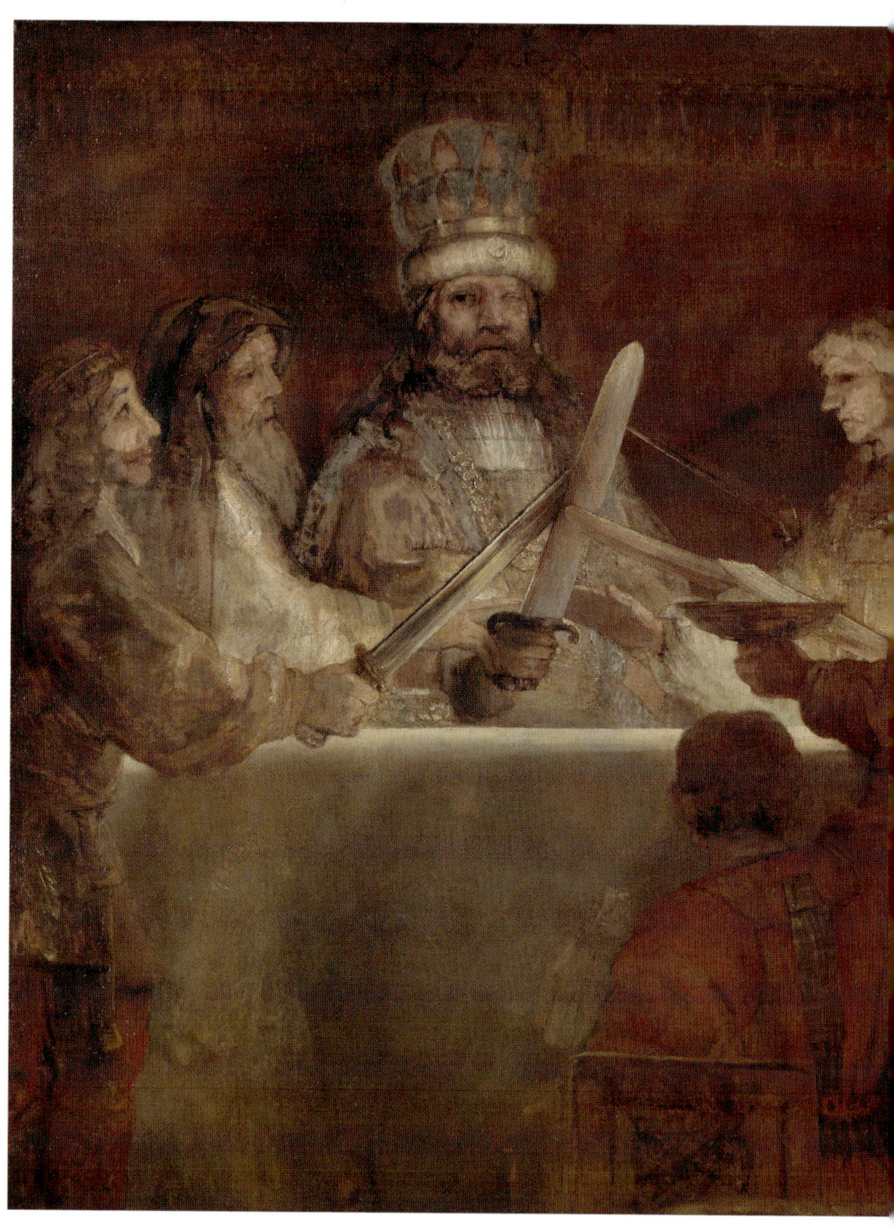

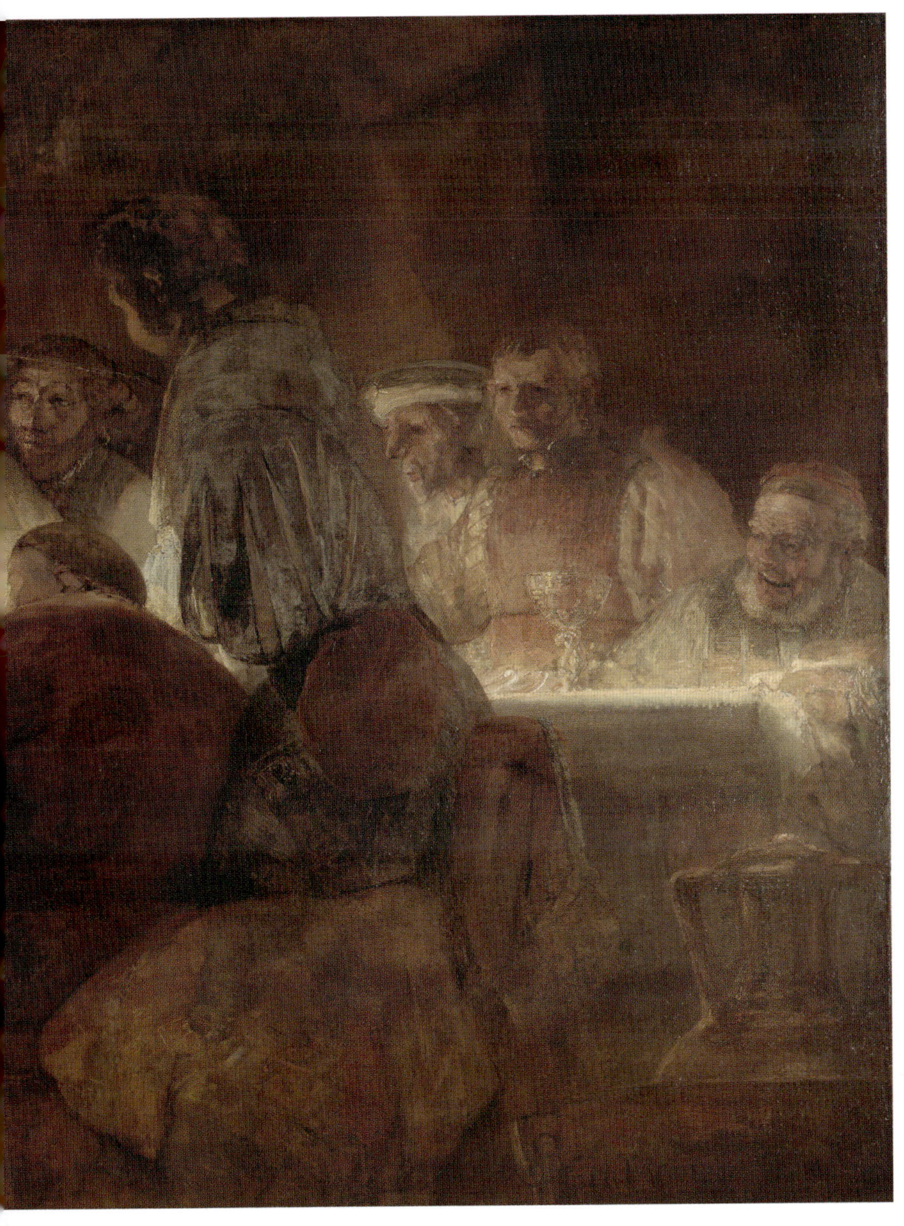

19 Rembrandt, *Oath of Claudius Civilis*, *c.* 1661–2, oil on canvas.

oath rather than clasp hands. Some figures are seen only from behind and below and one figure at the far end of the table is even leering. The broad late painting technique only underscores the roughness of these figures. But Rembrandt compounded his lack of decorum by returning to the literal text to display the missing left eye of Claudius. Even the crown that he bestows on the unattractive hero might have still offended the republican sensibilities of the city fathers of Amsterdam, who were always nervous about royal tyranny. And the Rembrandt image was out of phase with the more classical Roman presentations recently accepted from both Lievens and Jordaens as well as Flinck and Bol. Regardless of the reason, they rejected the painting and reassigned the commission in 1662 to an obscure, forgotten painter, another pupil of Rembrandt, named Jürgen Ovens, who followed the Flinck design.

The misfortune of Rembrandt's Amsterdam City Hall canvas reveals that even near the end of his career the painter still had ambitions consonant with the city's own assertiveness. Yet unlike his former pupils Flinck and Bol, he lacked the success with civic regents and patricians that would have assured him of ultimate success in portrait commissions. His initial popularity as a portraitist upon arriving in Amsterdam in 1631 – largely relying on the network of his dealer Hendrik Uylenburgh – lasted until the death of his wife Saskia in 1642, which also coincided with his completion of the *Nightwatch*. (There is no evidence, however, for the frequently repeated legend, including the Charles Laughton *Rembrandt* movie of 1936, which claims that Rembrandt's clients for that work were disappointed and precipitated his loss of clients and subsequent financial difficulties.) Yet Amsterdam sitters and groups still continued to figure, even in the later career of Rembrandt, when both individuals, pendants and the *Syndics* group portrait provided his essential livelihood.

TWO

Amsterdam's Religious Stew

HE DUTCH REVOLT BEGAN during the late 1560s as much in religious protest as in a political struggle for independence. Indeed, the Dutch likened their leader, the father of their country, martyred William of Orange (William 'the Silent'; d. 1584, assassinated by a Catholic loyalist), to Moses, leading his people out of bondage under a tyrannical pharaoh. In this case the modern pharaoh was King Philip II of Spain, who imposed his Catholicism as the state religion for his provinces of the Low Countries. Thus when the seven United Provinces of the Netherlands achieved de facto independence by the time of a truce in the conflict (1609–21), the new nation – while virulently anti-Catholic – emphatically turned away from a state religion altogether, despite a dominant Calvinist religion in the country in the form of the Dutch Reformed Church (first synod in August 1572). In May 1578, the militia of Amsterdam overthrew the standing, pro-Catholic city council and ousted local Catholic clergy, appropriated Catholic churches and cleansed the sanctuaries of images while suppressing Catholic worship. Despite some calls for religious tolerance, Catholicism could not be openly practised in the city (although 'secret' sanctuaries were maintained,

notably a chapel in the upper storeys of a canal house, 'Our Lord in the Attic', Onze Lieve Heer op Solder; now a museum). Nevertheless, other religious denominations were grudgingly permitted, including Lutherans, Mennonites and even Portuguese Jews, largely in flight from their repression in Iberian controlled regions.

In fact Calvinism itself was deeply riven by conflict – between the orthodox adherents of predestination and a less dogmatic, less determinist theology, championed by Leiden theologian Jacobus Arminius (d. 1609), thus often called Arminianism. During the 1570s and 1580s the doctrinaire Calvinist faction, striving for a restrictive state religion, was backed by regents and nobles and especially by the quasi-monarchical stadholder Maurits of Nassau (William the Silent's son and successor). Arminius also attracted influential allies, led in The Hague by court preacher Johannes Uytenbogaert (d. 1644), legal and religious scholar-jurist Hugo Grotius (d. 1645) and the Grand Pensionary (an executive office akin to being President of the Republic and Minister of Finance as well as Foreign Affairs), Johan van Oldenbarnevelt, another advocate of tolerance and freedom of conscience.

These theological conflicts over the stated Reformed Confession and catechism soon became political, which threatened not only the unity of the Reformed Church but that of the Dutch Republic, led to the brink of civil war over religion. Led by Uytenbogaert and backed by Oldenbarnevelt, in 1610 the Arminian party drew up a document, the 'Remonstrance', for the States General, proposing a revision of the Confession as well as an assertion of state authority over the Reformed

Church. Thereafter their faction, which eventually became an independent Church in its own right, was known as the 'Remonstrants'. Soon both orthodox Reformed preachers and the stadholder strove to impose central authority under the banner of Counter-Remonstrants. But the resulting tension between Maurits and Oldenbarnevelt reached such a pitch that the stadholder arrested the Grand Pensionary on charges of treason and had him executed on the block in May 1619. Grotius, the Pensionary of Rotterdam, was also arrested for treason in 1619, but he famously escaped from house arrest in a castle while hidden in a large book-chest in 1621, although he spent his remaining years in exile. In the meantime, a newly convened national Synod of Dort (Dordrecht) completed deliberations in 1619, reaffirming the dominant Counter-Remonstrant position, condemning the Remonstrants as heretics, and also endorsing a new translation into Dutch of Scripture, the States Bible (published in 1637).

Competition between religions during the Dutch Revolt provides the subject for Adriaen van de Venne's painting

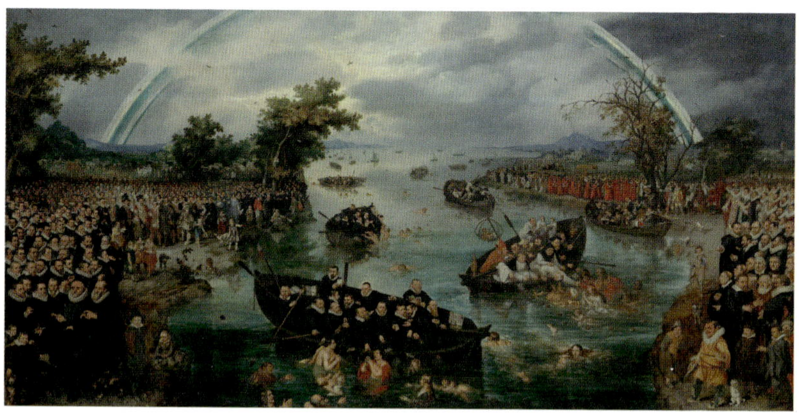

20 Adriaen van de Venne, *Fishing for Souls*, 1614, oil on panel.

of 1614, *Fishing for Souls* (illus. 20), which opposes Dutch Protestants against Flemish Catholics. In this allegory, each faith commands a boat on a river and casts its nets for new members of its flock. The Catholics on the far side include a bishop with his red cope and mitre, surrounded by plump monks, chiefly black-and-white-clad Dominicans. Beside the prayerful swimmers in the water by the Catholic boat appear a crucifix and a white mitre, but their numbers of converts remain distinctly smaller than the Evangelical catch. By contrast, the Protestants all dress in sober black garments with white collars as in conventional Dutch portraits, such as Rembrandt's own works of the early 1630s. Their nets reveal the theological virtues (in Latin) of Faith, Hope and Charity, and within their catch one even sees a Franciscan monk in his brown robes. Other boats with the same personnel appear in the distance, and the larger religious communities have assembled on their respective riverbanks. In the right distance, behind another boat with musicians (playing a viola da gamba, brass instruments and a portable organ), the Catholics stage a religious procession, vivid with the red robes of cardinals as they carry a pope on his ceremonial litter. They head towards a group of richly clad nobles, who stand before armed soldiers; at the head of the group stand portraits of the regents of the Southern Netherlands, Habsburg archdukes Albert (d. 1621) and Isabella (d. 1633), the princely patrons of Peter Paul Rubens. In the right corner of the foreground a court dwarf and a cross-eyed natural fool mark the assembled crowd as part of a royal hierarchy. By contrast, on the Protestant riverbank, many more figures crowd the shore, most of them soberly dressed; in their centre stands the stadholder, Maurits,

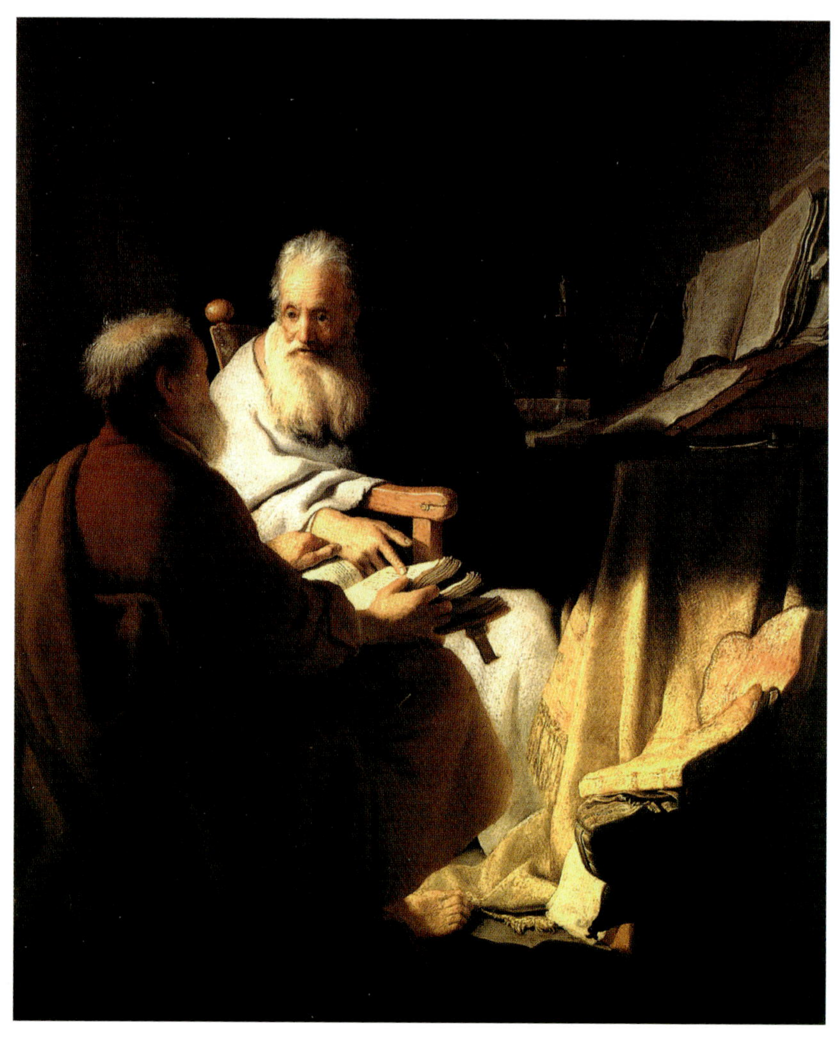

21 Rembrandt, *Two Scholars Disputing*, c. 1628, oil on panel.

wearing a black hat and bright red sleeves with a golden chain. Here even more individual portraits of Dutchmen fill the lower left corner. The painting as a whole is composed with relative balance under an overarching rainbow, but its point of view favours the Protestant side, subtly placing their boat nearest to the centre and closest to the viewer. Van de Venne (1589–1662) worked at Middelburg, near the border, and his painting conveys the current volatility of both religion and politics across the divide.

In one of Rembrandt's earliest paintings (*c.* 1628; illus. 21) two elderly, unidentified old men, clearly scholars in a well-used study, engage in lively disputation about the interpretation of a text. The frontal figure turns to his interlocutor to make a point with his fingers about the text in the open book, presumably Scripture, while the figure seen from behind marks several passages with his fingers to use in his response. Although these two humbly dressed men could be understood as ancient philosophers, presumably they are SS Peter and Paul, traditional pillars of the Church, but now the heads of contending spiritual factions: Peter, the first pope, represents Catholics; Paul, the great evangelist, sparks Protestant theology, interpreted as in this painting based on Scripture alone (*sola scriptura*). Only one moment in the Gospels (Galatians 1:18) notes the meeting of these two spiritual leaders (from the viewpoint of Paul), and a later verse (Galatians 2:16) clearly asserts the Pauline/Protestant doctrine of justification by faith rather than works. As if to suggest divine inspiration for this disputation, a strong light fills the room, falling on the open book and on the intimate dialogue of hands. Meanwhile, in the shadows a large globe suggests the world mission of the new faith, with high stakes for Christians in distant continents, such as the Portuguese and Dutch in Japan.

Half a decade later, Rembrandt painted a more experimental canvas (*c.* 1634; illus. 22), possibly intended for reproduction as an etching, which involves a truly global cast of characters. *John the Baptist Preaching* draws upon the passage (Luke 3:1–20; Matthew 3:1–12) about the 'voice crying in the wilderness' to both Temple officials and to a larger crowd. Again a strong pool of light falls on the figure of St John as well as the centre of his listeners. Rembrandt shows a hundred listeners, comprising a diverse population as well as diverse responses to the Gospel message. Ranging widely in age, sex and class, they include figures in exotic costumes from Asia and Africa as well as a camel. Such foreigners indicate not only emerging Dutch trade interests in those continents through the Dutch East India Company (VOC), but potentially wider ambitions – a tall Native American appears in his feather headdress behind the Baptist, and an armed, turban-clad Ottoman warrior at the right-hand edge.

Yet St John also attacks the Sadducees and Pharisees in his audience as a 'brood of vipers', so in the lower centre of the image, at the very edge of the light, Rembrandt also includes a trio of Jews, marked by their distinctive kaftan robes and headgear. These elders also wear accurately rendered Hebrew letters on their robes, which excerpt Old Testament lines that declare their own faith (Deuteronomy 6:5–8); thus, they pointedly turn away from the preacher and discuss his message with hostility. This early image of Jews by Rembrandt is both informed and negative, like that of Paul himself, who in

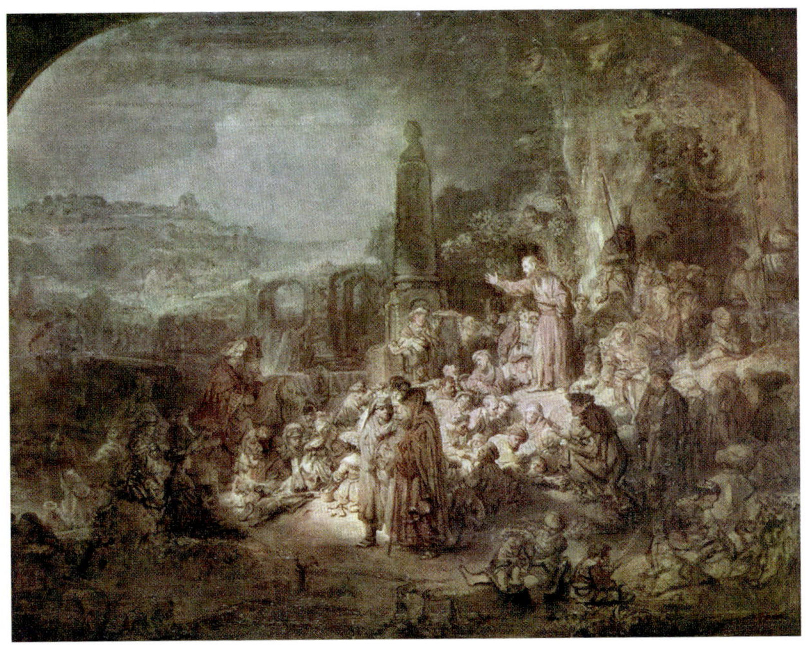

this part of the painting seems to embody the warning of the Baptist: 'Do not begin to say to yourselves, "We have Abraham as our father."' Rembrandt would live in a Jewish neighbourhood in Amsterdam and would engage sympathetically with both the Old Testament and with several of his current neighbours, but in the context of New Testament revelation, he clearly saw the senior religion as a relic of the past.

No documentation certifies Rembrandt's own religious beliefs, although he was married in the Dutch Reformed church, baptized his children in it and was buried in a grave of the Westerkerk in Amsterdam. But his affiliation seems less important than his close reading of Scripture, surely abetted by the appearance after 1637 of the *Statenbijbel* (Dutch

22 Rembrandt, *John the Baptist Preaching*, c. 1634, oil on canvas.

State Bible). Religious leaders appear only occasionally among his portraits, and their own range of affiliations undermines any secure sense of the artist's own beliefs, since many of those sitters commissioned their likenesses, often as etchings for wider distribution.

Around the time of *John the Baptist Preaching*, Rembrandt made a pair of portraits of Johannes Uytenbogaert, the leading Remonstrant, who had fled to Antwerp to avoid the fate of Oldenbarnevelt and Grotius, only to return to Holland in 1625. That year was not accidental; he had tutored the younger half-brother of the stadholder Maurits, after whose death Frederik Hendrik became his successor, so a safe return was assured for Uytenbogaert. Nevertheless, he resumed an active religious role in The Hague, again pursuing tolerance and freedom of conscience. By 1630 Remonstrants had founded their first church in Amsterdam and established an Amsterdam Athenaeum in 1634, led by Simon Episcopius.

On the occasion of a visit to Amsterdam through the invitation of a wealthy Remonstrant candle merchant, Abraham Anthoniszoon, Uytenbogaert sat for a painted portrait by Rembrandt (1633), where the theologian stands at three-quarter length and turns from his left towards the viewer, seemingly spontaneously, hand on heart. That gesture suggests a kind of steadfast faith, to both the Bible text and the Arminian community. Behind Uytenbogaert an open Bible on a lectern shows his serious religious study, but beside the Bible his large black hat also suggests a busy, peripatetic life. Warm light glows on both face and hands as well as on the book and silhouettes dark robes and the crowning theologian's skullcap. Crisp details define aged skin in face and hands as well as a lace collar, like other Rembrandt portraits of the early 1630s in Amsterdam, seen earlier. Using the same formula, in 1634 Rembrandt also painted a dual portrait of a Reformed minister: Johannes Elison of Norwich, seated as a husband beside his wife, Maria Bockenolle, both of them full length and life-sized. Elison in his skullcap and dark robes also holds his hand on his heart and sits within a book-lined study with an open Bible beside him.

When Rembrandt produced a subsequent etched portrait of Uytenbogaert (1635; illus. 23), it bore a handwritten Latin inscription written by Grotius, a eulogy for the sitter and an appreciation of his sufferings in exile as a caption:

> The worldly court was obliged to condemn the man
> so admired by the pious, the soldiers, and the court
> itself, and to denounce his convictions. [Oh] Hague,
> after much wandering your fellow townsman returns
> to [you], withered, not by years alone.

The period of the mid-1630s brought even more suffering to the sitter, since Frederik Hendrik now sided with the Counter-Remonstrants and also renewed conflict with the Spanish Netherlands. Rembrandt's heavily modelled, careful etching places Uytenbogaert at half-length, seated behind a desk, again with a large open book before him and a cluster of other books at his elbow. His dress is scholarly, an academic robe trimmed with fur, again complemented with a skullcap. His gaze is resolute. Presumably with the Grotius tribute, this print would have circulated to the friends and supporters of the Remonstrant leader.

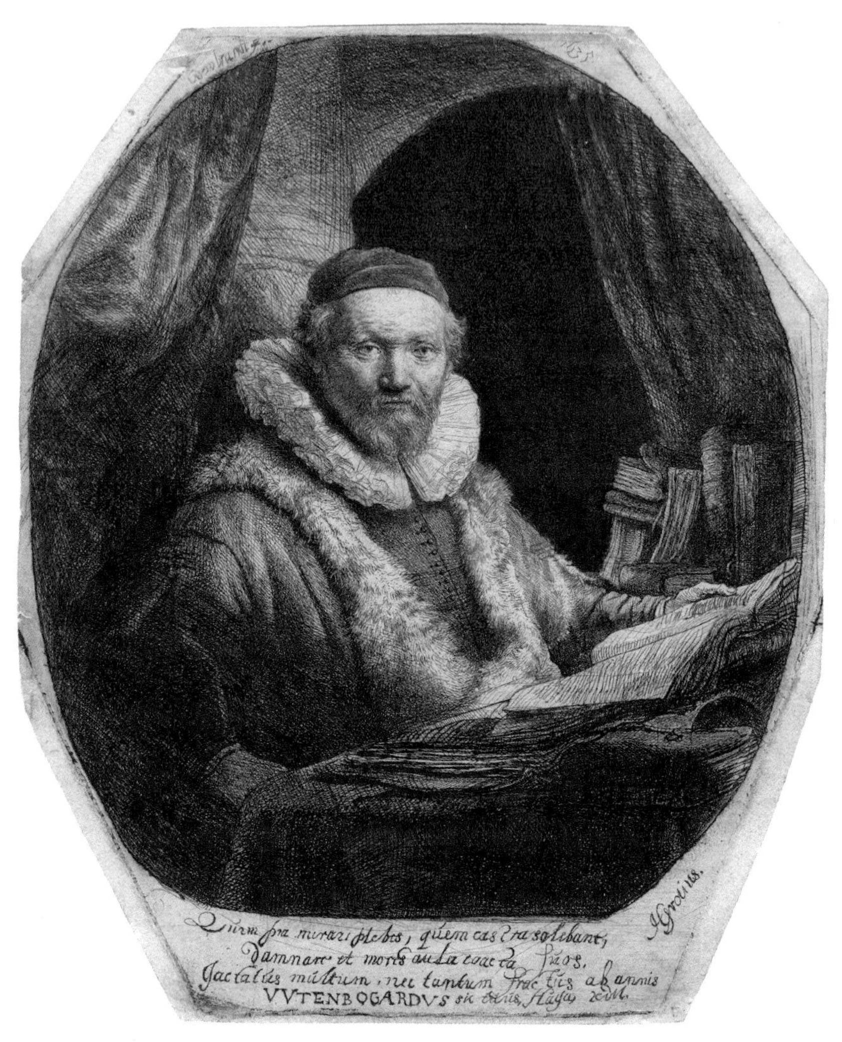

23 Rembrandt, *Johannes Uytenbogaert*, 1635, etching.

Early in the 1640s Rembrandt produced another large-scale husband-and-wife portrait of a religious leader, but this time on a single large canvas rather than as a pair of pendants like the Elisons. This commission (1641; illus. 24) came from a renowned orator and lay preacher, a Mennonite, but also a cloth merchant, Cornelis Claesz Anslo. Rembrandt began the project with a careful ink drawing (first sketched in black chalk) at full length (1640), possibly revealing an original plan for pendant portraits. The drawing composition shows the preacher at his desk, wearing a hat along with his fur-lined scholarly robe. He is turned to his left to gesture rhetorically, as if in explanation of the open Bible text he has been studying. Seen at half-length but now viewed from below, that same posture carries over into the large canvas, where Anslo turns to his wife, Aaltje Gerritsdr. Schouten, in an interaction that unites the two figures on the large single canvas (compare the 1632 Gardner double portrait, illus. 7).

The setting is another book-lined study, and now the carpet-covered desk with several volumes fills half the canvas, to underscore the spiritual emphasis on the text practised by this highly observant Waterlander Mennonite. Aaltje's garments are conservative and modest in comparison to the collars and cuffs seen in Rembrandt's portraits of prosperous ladies. She listens attentively to the pious words of her husband, distractedly gazing past him while lost in reflective thought. Both figures enact Mennonite doctrine that emphasizes inner faith and personal inspiration, possibly suggested in the portrait by the candlestick-holder on the desk, which balances the upright figure of Anslo.

Here the Renaissance portrait convention of the 'speaking likeness' emerges more emphatically for Anslo than for Uytenbogaert, perhaps because of Anslo's fame as a preacher. Rembrandt took up the challenge to depict that rhetorical force, but he faced in a still portrait the same dilemma as faced by Albrecht Dürer in his portraits of leading religious reformers of the early sixteenth century, such as Erasmus or Luther's lieutenant Philipp Melanchthon; on their prints he modestly alluded to the power of the word over the image by including inscriptions, such as the one accompanying Erasmus: 'A better portrait his writings show.' Indeed, this Rembrandt portrait elicited a sparring match with the leading

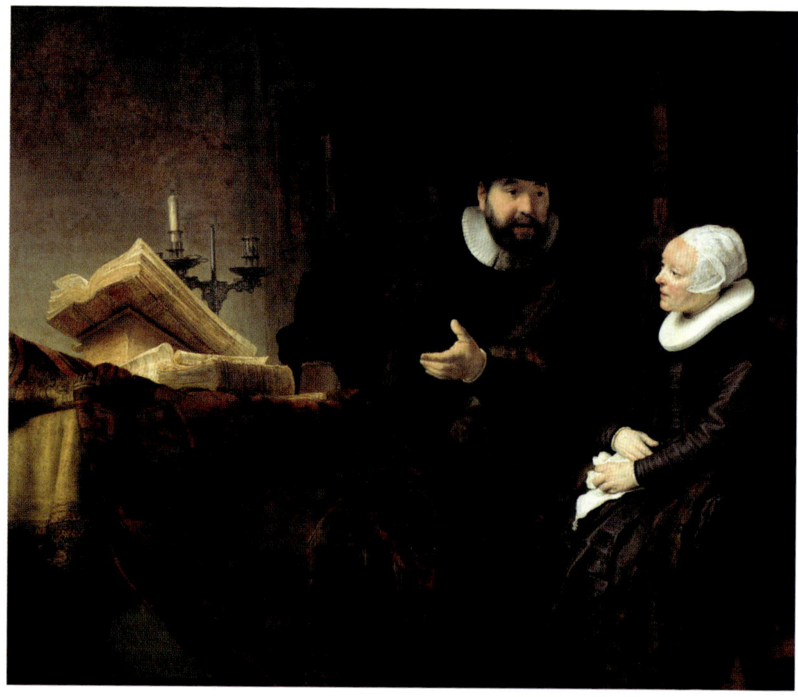

24 Rembrandt, *Cornelis Anslo and Aaltje Gerritsdr. Schouten*, 1641, oil on canvas.

poet-playwright of Amsterdam, Joost van den Vondel, who penned a verse of challenge in the perennial competition between word and image:

> Aye, Rembrandt, paint Cornelis's voice,
> The visible part is the least of him:
> The invisible can only be known through the ears.
> He who would see Anslo must hear him.

But another Latin verse by Remonstrant poet Caspar Barlaeus also pays tribute to both Anslo and to the Rembrandt portrait. Its final lines assert that the preacher is the epitome of piety:

> exemplary for the Dutch.
> So is Anslo depicted; his piety manifests itself
> So that perchance he in old age should cease to
>   speak,
> His likeness could speak to the people.

Anslo, however, wanted more from the artist and commissioned an etched solo portrait (1641; illus. 25). This renewed emphasis on his portrait raises the paradox that a preacher of the Word insisted so strongly on his personal image. Yet a century-long tradition of portrait prints of celebrated Mennonite preachers already extended back to the Anabaptist period of the 1530s in Germany. For this second project Rembrandt submitted another drawing, in red chalk with highlights and corrections in white, uncharacteristically signed and dated 1640. Rembrandt also incised the outline

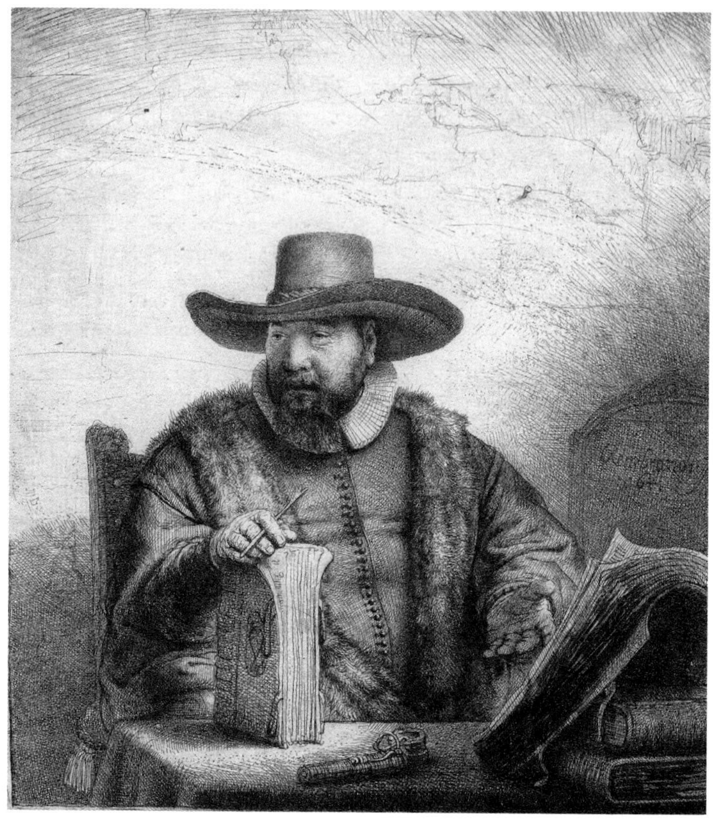

of the drawing for transfer, so the printed image in exact size reverses the original orientation of the drawing. Several small changes represent Anslo anew: he sits behind his desk, and now he grips a pen in his hand, which rests upon one closed book, perhaps his own work. But still he gestures with the same open hand before a large open tome that rests atop other books. A framed painting (or a mirror?) conspicuously turned to the wall carries the artist's name and date, and Rembrandt has added an illusionistic nail protruding from

25 Rembrandt, *Preacher Cornelis Anslo*, 1641, etching.

the otherwise empty wall behind the preacher; presumably both items allude further to Anlo's self-imposed austerity (although he still wears the same hat and fur-trimmed robe). A denial of painting might also accord with Mennonite beliefs in the primacy of God's Word over religious images.

Rembrandt's connections with Mennonites of various denominations surely began with his association during the previous decade by Hendrick Uylenburgh, his early entrepreneurial dealer in Amsterdam, who was also a Waterlander. So evident were the painter's links to that religious affiliation that his Danish pupil Bernhard Keil (*c.* 1642–4) noted to Filippo Baldinucci in Italy that Rembrandt himself was a Mennonite (for a 1686 biography published in an early history of graphics). But no further documentation corroborates this claim, and Rembrandt's lively engagement with biblical illustration, including Old Testament stories, runs against the grain of Mennonite piety.

Much more personal is Rembrandt's final image of a clergyman who is also a relative by marriage: the 1646 etching of Jan Cornelisz. Sylvius (illus. 26), family guardian of his wife Saskia. Sylvius served Reformed congregations in Friesland, where he married Saskia's cousin; he stood proxy at her 1632 engagement and witness to the baptism of their first two children. He successfully served in Amsterdam at the Old Church (Oude Kerk) amid fierce conflicts between Reformed and Remonstrant factions and 'preached the holy word for forty-five years', according to the print.

Rembrandt had already sealed the family tie with an earlier etched portrait (1633; B. 266) of Sylvius, whose scholar-in-his-study half-length echoes the *Uytenbogaert* of the same year but with a bit more intimacy and empathy for the figure, seen more closely with folded hands above his open book. His slightly downcast eyes provide the suggestion of pious reflection. No inscription identifies the sitter, in contrast to the *Uytenbogaert*, so this print might have had a more limited, chiefly family, circulation.

Far more accomplished and dramatic is the larger 1646 *Sylvius* etching, a posthumous tribute (the sitter died in 1638 at age 74, as noted on the print). The format of the portrait adopts a convention of painted and printed portraits in oval portholes, especially from the Haarlem circles of Frans Hals, whose oval portraits of Reverend Johannes Acronius (1627) and Johannes Bogardus (1628; painting lost) were both etched by Jan van de Velde II. Simulating a stone tablet, this format is particularly appropriate for a posthumous portrait, because it derives from ancient Roman *imagines clipeata* ('shield portraits'), also still evoked in Rome for contemporary memorials by Gian Lorenzo Bernini (such as his celebrated tomb image for Maria Raggi, Santa Maria sopra Minerva, 1643). Once again, Rembrandt prepared the compositional layout of the etching with an ink drawing, where the oval format and the shading from below was worked out along with the basic hand gesture of the sitter and its shadow, to be reversed in printing.

In this case the artist extended the earlier home-made inscription in honour of Uytenbogaert with a professionally executed calligraphic flourish to render a fulsome Latin eulogy by Barlaeus, which extols both the oratory but also the exemplary life of the preacher:

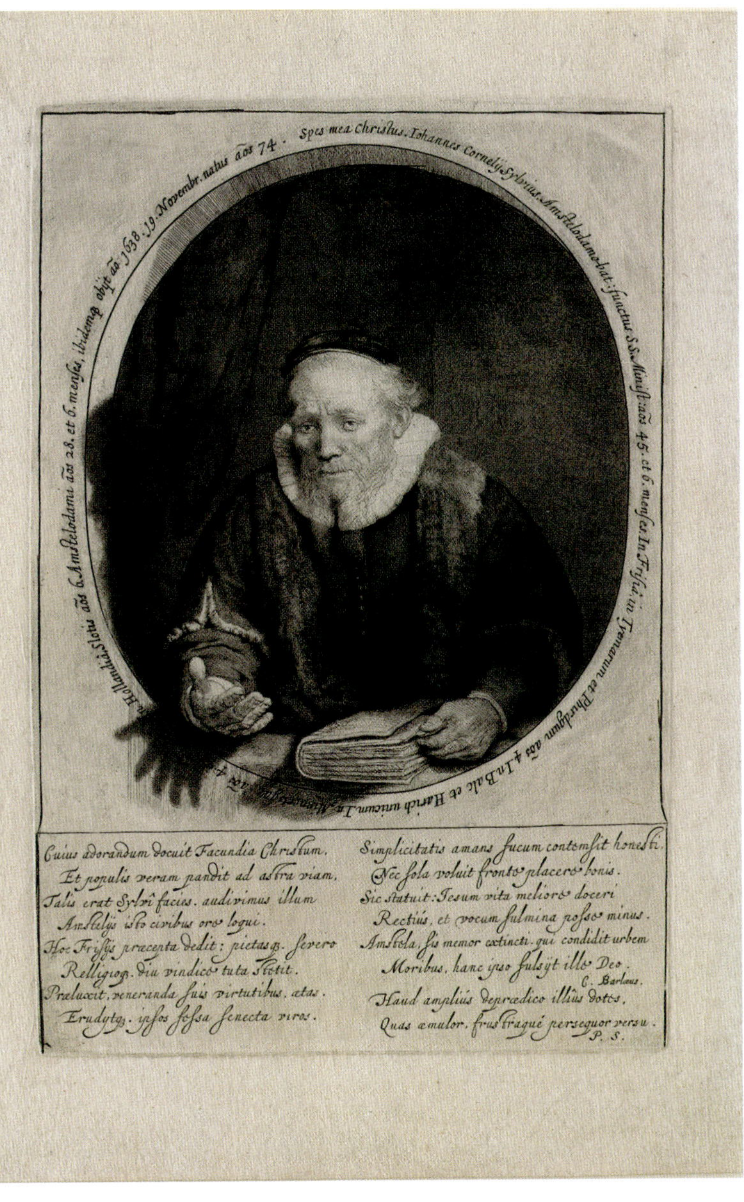

26 Rembrandt, *Jan Cornelisz. Sylvius*, posthumous portrait, 1646, etching.

This is how Sylvius looked – he whose eloquence
    taught men to honour Christ
And showed them the true path to heaven.
We all heard him when with these lips
He preached to the citizens of Amsterdam . . .
Jesus can be better taught
By living the right life
Than by raising the voice.

In full mastery of printmaking, Rembrandt admixes his etching with fine engraved and drypoint lines. His superb sense of lighting allows him to show the dark cast shadow on the fictive surface of the oval frame, caused by the dramatically foreshortened rhetorical hand gesture (echoing both the *Nightwatch* and the two earlier Anslo portraits), which seems to extend out into viewer space. A second shadow is cast by the book in his left hand, presumably a Bible, with passages for comparison indexed by fingers at their pages (compare illus. 21, above). Finally, the profile of the preacher appears in shadow at the left edge of the oval. In effect, the godly minister is addressing viewers of the print fashioned in his memory and honour. This memorial print, expressly addressed – and in Latin verses – to the citizens of Amsterdam, makes a public, formal and largely ecumenical religious statement.

REMBRANDT AND THE BIBLE

Both in paintings and prints as well as in hosts of drawings (many of which surely have not survived), Rembrandt is justly celebrated for his engagement with figures and tales from the Bible, both Old and New Testaments. His narratives reveal that he was a close reader of Scripture, including some apocryphal texts not even part of the Calvinist canon, such as the Book of Tobit and the stories of Bel and the Dragon or Susanna and the Elders, both appended to the Book of Daniel. Some of his inspiration derived from the model of his Amsterdam teacher, Pieter Lastman (*c.* 1583–1633), a Catholic (in Rome in 1605), whose historical references to biblical settings and costumes as well as classicizing features were recurrent touchstones for Rembrandt across his own career.

Rembrandt's first dated work, a *Stoning of St Stephen* (1625), shows a predictable early dependence on Lastman (whose lost 1619 version of the same subject survives in a drawn copy) for its setting, costumes and active figures. His choice of theme (Acts 7:58–60) might have been occasioned by the internecine religious conflicts within the Reformed Church, whose epicentre was the university faculty of Leiden, home town of Rembrandt; the torments of the saint might be thus compared to the ongoing persecution of Remonstrants at the hands of their former co-religionists. Among the figures in the mob of attackers we discern several possible self-portraits of Rembrandt. This image of the artist as witness-participant in a Christian saint's martyrdom publicly asserts his personal sense of sinfulness and guilt. This distinctive kind of affective piety had characterized late medieval meditations on the details of the Passion and other evocative Gospel moments; moreover, the sixteenth century brought both the *Spiritual Exercises* of Ignatius Loyola for Jesuit Catholic meditation along with widespread Protestant emphasis on emotional internalization of religious events, made newly accessible by translations of the Bible into vernacular languages (for example, the King James Bible and the Dutch *Statenbijbel*). From the very first images, then, Rembrandt professed his sincere Christian beliefs in public display.

A similar personal engagement also marked another of Rembrandt's ambitious early religious works, produced first as a painting but soon reproduced as a large-scale, detailed etching. *The Descent from the Cross* (1633; illus. 27) replicates a painting (1632/3; Munich, Alte Pinakothek), which Rembrandt had recently produced for the stadholder Frederik Hendrik. But even though Rembrandt was already becoming an accomplished etcher of dramatic Gospel scenes (compare his recent *Raising of Lazarus* from the previous year, B. 73), to produce this finely detailed print he hired a professional print collaborator: engraver Jan van Vliet (c. 1600/10–1688). Remarkable details – of lighting, including shafts of light from the heavens against the nocturne, of background buildings, and of details in faces and costumes – all stem from Van Vliet.

The idea to replicate a painting for wider circulation and publicity comes from Rembrandt's older rival from Catholic Flanders, Peter Paul Rubens, who hired a team of professional engravers to reproduce some of his most celebrated pictures as prints, religious as well as mythological and even including landscapes at a later moment. Indeed, starting with Raphael and then Titian in sixteenth-century Italy, one of the hallmarks of a prestigious painter was his generation of prints, engraved reproductions of his celebrated compositions: Rubens was following this model, and Rembrandt in turn initially sought to follow Rubens with the *Descent from*

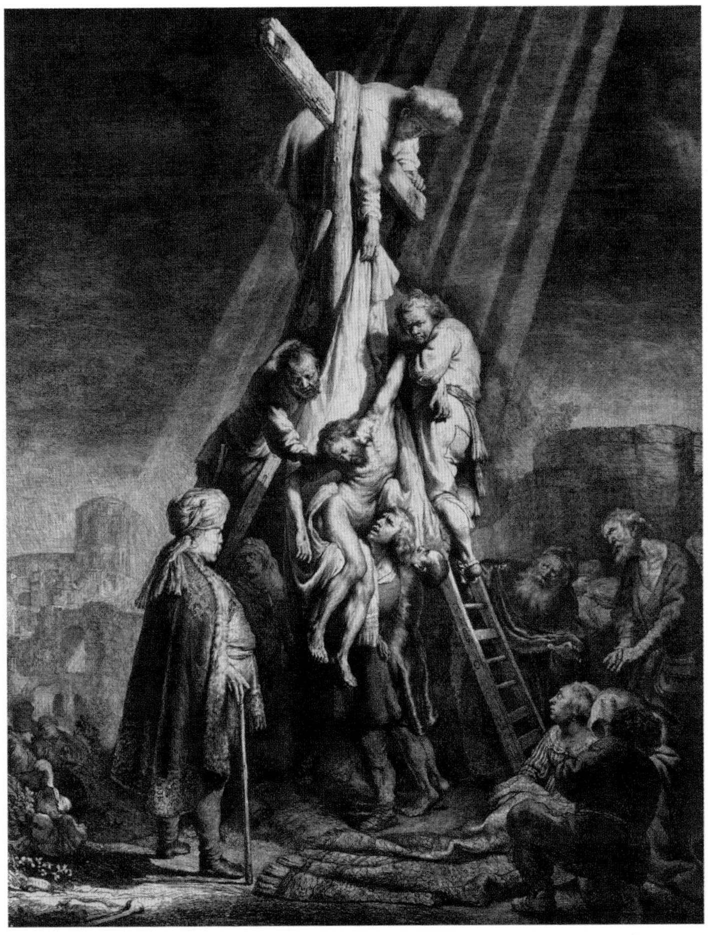

the Cross. Rubens's own *Descent from the Cross* (1611–12) was a commission from the Antwerp Guild of the Arquebusiers (the equivalent militia group to Rembrandt's own *Nightwatch* commission, but entirely focused on religious imagery for an altarpiece connected to the theme of bearing the body of Jesus). Rubens's own engraving of the *Descent* was produced

27 Rembrandt (with Jan van Vliet), *Descent from the Cross*, 1633, etching.

recently (in 1630) by Lucas Vorsterman, and likely served as Rembrandt's immediate stimulus.

But Rubens's massive, muscular body of Christ as a spiritual athlete almost hovers in the centre of the composition, the brightest and largest figure in the image, fully surrounded by handsome followers. In contrast, Rembrandt's Christ is a broken body, limply sagging and heavy on the shoulders of much scruffier apostle figures. Jesus's nakedness is exposed without Rubens's decorous loincloth, and his head hangs downward awkwardly below his upraised shoulder despite being placed in the compositional centre. Christ's hyperextended left arm has lost all its power and bends limply in the hands of one follower on a ladder, who struggles to control the downward droop of the corpse.

Close inspection, especially of the engraving (not as clear in the Munich painting), reveals that the frowning face of that same apostle is Rembrandt's own. In the *Descent from the Cross*, he numbers himself among the followers of Christ, sharing the pain of martyrdom rather than imposing it. Even more strikingly, in the companion painting, the *Raising of the Cross* (never engraved), Rembrandt appears in a blue beret at the foot of the cross and in the bright centre of the composition as a principal instigator of the Crucifixion, a henchman rather than a compassionate co-sufferer. Far more than as a signature or marker of his personal stake in the imagery, Rembrandt here makes a self-conscious statement of faith – that Christians bear responsibility through their sins for the torments of Christ (a concept called the 'Perpetual Passion') but that they can also be loyal followers, emotionally linked to the scene as if they were witnesses.

Contemporary verses of devotion by Reformed poets in Dutch express similar sentiments. For example, Jeremias de Decker's 'Good Friday' contains a confessional tone that conveys both consciousness of sin and empathetic response to the Passion:

Since on this mournful day no comic strain
But tragic note should rise:
O Lord, I now must mourn your bitter pain
And [through it] for my sin be moved to sighs.

And Constantijn Huygens, Rembrandt's early supporter and intermediary with the stadholder for these very Passion pictures, had translated the devotional poetry of John Donne, such as 'Good Friday, 1613. Riding Westward', during the 1620s. Donne's *cri de cœur* includes the following outburst to cleanse his sins: 'O thinke mee worth thine anger, punish mee.'

Rembrandt, however, never continued his plan to reproduce his paintings, and his anticipated cycle of New Testament subjects for the stadholder became sporadic in delivery and was never followed up. But a rare letter from the painter to his patron Huygens suggests the kind of effects that he sought in his religious works. In February 1636 Rembrandt writes about his diligent preparation completing the three Passion pictures for the stadholder: an Entombment, a Resurrection (both half-finished) and an Ascension (completed). In a follow-up letter to Huygens in 1639, Rembrandt expressed his desire to paint a picture with the 'greatest and most natural emotion/motion' ('die meeste ende die naetuereelste beweechgelickheijt'), where the last word can indicate both motion

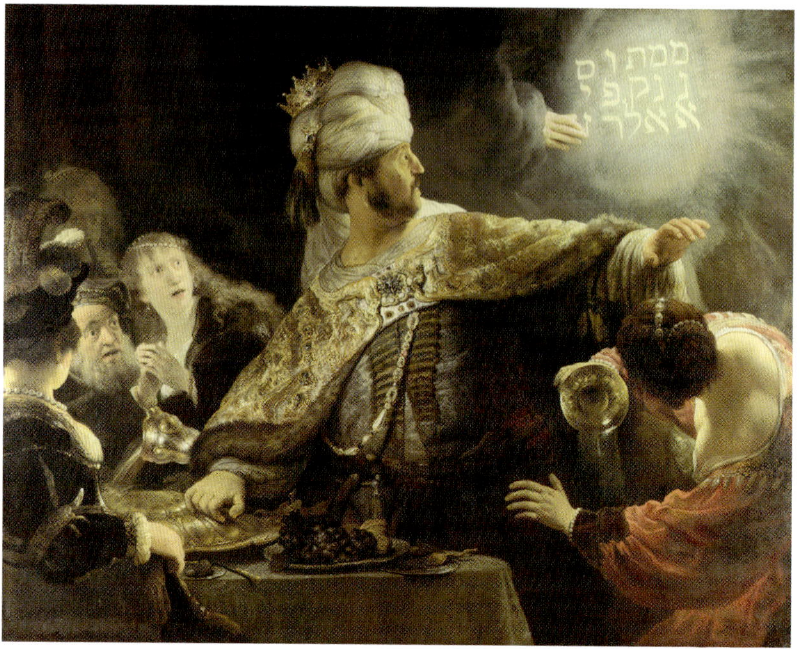

and emotion, a point debated by interpreters. For Rembrandt, however, the two were linked, just as Leonardo da Vinci spoke of 'motions of the mind' for narratives, conveyed through body gestures and facial expressions. Significantly, the religious paintings by Rembrandt during his early maturity in the 1630s are action-filled with characters who boldly emote through broad gestures. He also seems to have planned for more etchings, perhaps in collaboration with Van Vliet, who also translated an oil sketch of *Christ Presented to the People* (1634) into another detailed engraving, even larger; but Rembrandt also prepared several other monochrome (grisaille) small studies around this same moment, including the Berlin *John the Baptist Preaching*.

28 Rembrandt, *Belshazzar's Feast*, c. 1635, oil on canvas.

Rembrandt dramatizes the climax of an Old Testament religious scene in his *Belshazzar's Feast* (c. 1635; illus. 28). Rich descriptions of costume, still-life elements and lighting all reinforce the powerful facial expressions and theatrical poses of the figures. At the centre of the composition a ruler clad in magnificent brocade robes and with an exotic crowned turban starts back in amazement. Around him on either side both forward-facing and backward-facing figures gape with the same astonishment; one of them is frozen in the midst of pouring wine from a golden pitcher. They all are observing a supernatural event, as a detached divine finger writes on a well a warning in Hebrew characters (accurately transcribed by Rembrandt). The scene represents a moment (Daniel 5) when Belshazzar, king of Babylon, is feasting in Jerusalem with the precious vessels looted from the holy Temple of the Jews. That divine message alerts Belshazzar that because of his blasphemy 'God has numbered the days of your kingdom and brought it to an end; you have been weighed in the balance and found wanting.' Further, the message prophesies that his kingdom will be divided between the Medes and the Persians (under Cyrus the Great), who were even then besieging Jerusalem. Belshazzar will die before the night is out.

Only the young prophet Daniel could read the Hebrew letters, not only because of their characters but because they are to be read vertically instead of horizontally. This ingenious solution to the problem of why the inscription could not be read derives from the theory of a contemporary Jewish rabbi, Menasseh ben Israel, whose house was across the street from Rembrandt in the Breestraat area. His discussion of the warning appeared in his 1639 publication, *De terminis vitae libri tres*, a few years after Rembrandt's painting. This pre-publication solution for the artwork indicates that Rembrandt must have consulted with the rabbi for both the Hebrew orthography and the layout of the inscription itself. We also recall in this context that the Hebrew letters on the garments of the Jews in *John the Baptist Preaching* are also accurate enough to be read in comparison to modern Hebrew Bibles with the same passage.

By tradition, a 1636 etched portrait by Rembrandt of a man with a broad-brimmed hat in an oval has been identified with Menasseh ben Israel, but recent scholarship has pointed to a different portrait of Menasseh by Jewish artist and engraver Salom Italia to argue against that identity (Italia's linework is cruder, but his figure is thinner, and his facial hair is both thicker and better groomed). A painted portrait of Rembrandt's now-unknown sitter was also made by his pupil Govaert Flinck in 1637, but his age, listed as 44, differs from Menasseh's age of 33 in the same year. Rembrandt did make a later portrait etching of a known Jewish patron, physician and poet, Ephraim Bueno (see illus. 15).

Two other painted portraits by Rembrandt of men with skullcaps has often associated them with Jews in the Amsterdam community (1648; 1663), but as we have seen, skullcaps were also worn by pious preachers in the Netherlands (and apparently in the seventeenth century such headwear was not obligatory for pious Jews). Neither painting seems to be a serious commissioned portrait of a prominent sitter, however, so the possibility remains strong that these are studies of actual, anonymous figures from the Jewish neighbourhood

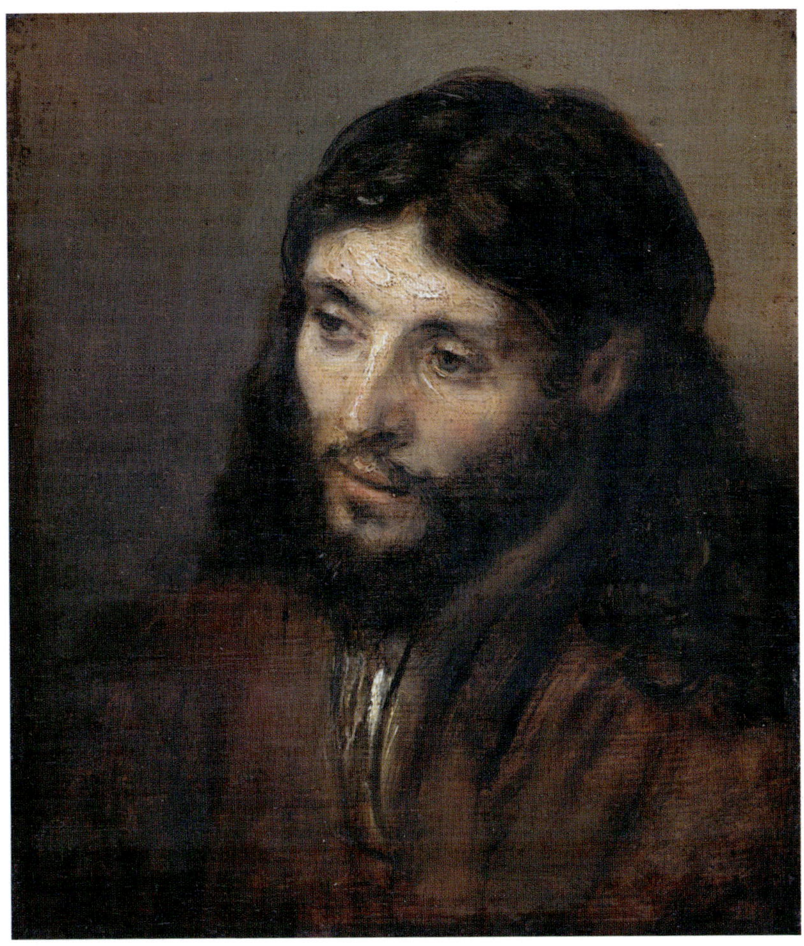

around Breestraat, possibly for later use as types within Rembrandt's religious crowds of listeners.

In fact, Rembrandt did produce several study head (or *tronie*) paintings of the *Head of Jesus*; the finest of these is in Berlin (*c.* 1650; illus. 29), but eight or nine other versions exist in various states of condition, variously attributed to either

29 Rembrandt, *Head of Jesus, c.* 1650, oil on panel.

the master or the workshop. Debate also swirls around these heads, concerning whether Rembrandt had a live model, presumably a long-haired Jew from his own Breestraat neighbourhood. The very fact that so many versions of the figure exist seems to preclude that many individual sittings for each one, although an actual model might have inspired some initial picture. Certainly by this period Rembrandt had already painted his own imagined version of the head of Christ for a couple of decades, most recently in his 1648 *Supper at Emmaus* (Paris, Louvre; a workshop version of the same year is in Copenhagen). Indeed, scholars have often associated the long-haired face studies of the head of Jesus with the figure found in the Louvre *Emmaus*.

Ambiguity of these head studies underscores their significance. They look precisely as if they were portraits, posed informally from life with varying angles of lighting and head turns; their facial expressions seem spontaneous and persuasive. Particularly by avoiding the permanence and immobility of a symmetrical frontal pose or profile, like an icon, what Rembrandt has done with these images of Jesus is to depict him as if alive and present, fully human and with all the animated variety of an actor. Increasingly Rembrandt's religious pictures in the latter half of his career, beginning in the late 1640s, began to focus less on the physical activity and broad gestures of his characters and increasingly on their internal mental states and character, conveyed, as here, chiefly by face and eyes.

One of Rembrandt's most elaborate Gospel narratives, full of figures like the *Preaching of John the Baptist*, is his etching now known as the *Hundred-guilder Print* (c. 1648/9; illus. 30)

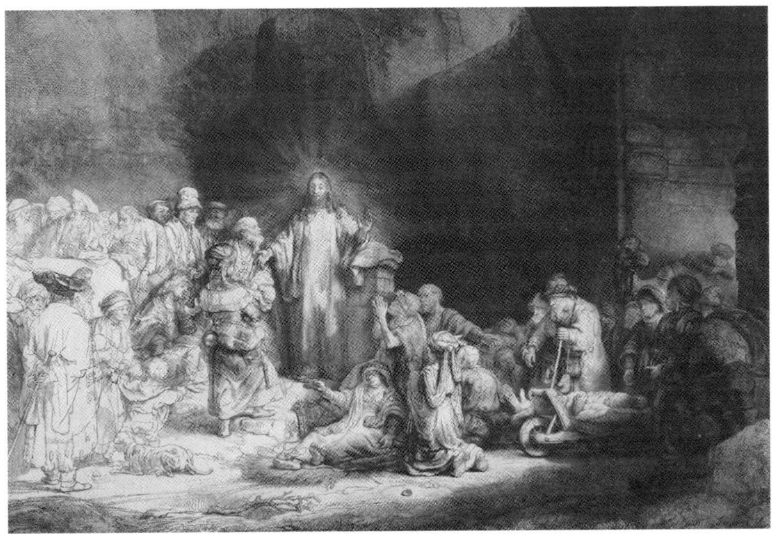

due to a high price for its early valuation. What this image represents is a series of events from Matthew 19: healing the sick; welcoming children as the epitome of unconditional faith and love ('Let the little children come to me', Matthew 19:14); rebuking a rich man for his possessions; but also instructing the disciples, who appear above the right hand of Christ. Instead of the more traditional imagery of the Infancy or Passion of Jesus at either end of his life on earth, Rembrandt instead shows Jesus on his mission, actively teaching, preaching and healing.

This long-haired face of Jesus already anticipates the Berlin study head and its echoes, but with a more slender vis-age and an explicit supernatural halo against the etched dark shadows behind him. (As a printmaker, Rembrandt begins here to utilize mixed intaglio tools, so that rougher drypoint outlines contrasts of contours and hatched shadows.) Certainly

30 Rembrandt, *'Hundred-guilder Print' Christ Preaching and Healing*, c. 1648/9, etching.

in this composition, Jesus stands at the centre as the tallest figure, the culmination of a pyramid of seekers, variously rendered in nuanced detail or in outline – young and old, rich and poor, followers and even antagonists. (At the left edge a group of elderly Pharisees pointedly turn away from his message and confer together.)

Even a camel appears under the gateway to the right, clearly alluding to the parable verse: 'It is easier for a camel to go through the eye of a needle than for a rich man to enter the kingdom of God' (Matthew 19:24). The object of this lesson also appears in the print in the form of a seated young man at left, surrounded by mothers and children, who puts his hand over his mouth in seeming distress at the words of Jesus. His situation might have held particular poignancy for the artist in the late 1640s, when his own financial fortunes began to sour, eventuating in his declaration of bankruptcy in 1656.

Like a number of Rembrandt prints, this one seems to tiptoe around theological controversies that divided denominations in seventeenth-century Holland. Particularly sensitive was the question of infant baptism, rejected by Mennonites but sanctioned by Calvinists in the Reformed Church and earlier by Lutherans. With images of Jesus blessing the young children, strictly according to Scripture, either party could feel justified. In similar fashion, Rembrandt's 1639 etching the *Death of the Virgin* seems to balance Protestant views with Catholic ones, as it emphasizes her physical ageing despite the welcome of a heavenly host above. Moreover, despite the presence of a mitred priest at the bedside, this death occurs without the details of Catholic last rites (Extreme Unction) or any indications of the Coronation of the Virgin, a frequent Catholic image of Mary's ultimate destiny. Thus Rembrandt seems to have deliberately temporized in the details of his religious images, especially prints, in order to operate safely within theologically contested issues and to reach the widest possible audience. He even produced other etchings that drew on a more expressly Catholic tradition: prints of both St Francis (1657; B. 107) and St Jerome (numerous) as well as Madonna images, the *Virgin and Child in the Clouds* (1641; B. 61) or Mary as *Mater Dolorosa with the Instruments of the Passion* (*c.* 1652; B. 85).

Rembrandt's ongoing involvement with the Old Testament continued into his late paintings, such as his large *Moses with the Tablets of the Law* (1659; illus. 31). Here again the 'thou shalt nots' of the final five Commandments are all rendered in accurate Hebrew. The Ten Commandments had assumed greater religious significance in Holland after Calvinists banned religious imagery from their churches; indeed, many Dutch sanctuaries even substituted boards on their altars with the literal words, in Dutch, of the Commandments. Dutch Calvinists often defined themselves in historical terms as modern Israelites, who escaped from the pharaonic oppression of Catholic king Philip II of Spain. Moreover, Calvin himself valued the covenant of God with Abraham and the Jewish people of the Old Testament as a prior, partial revelation, before the advent of Jesus. In fact, here too Calvinists aligned more closely with Jewish concepts, because in contrast to Catholics, they adopted as the first Commandment the initial wording of the Exodus passage that 'You shall have no other gods besides Me' (Exodus 20:2–3). Thus Rembrandt's

Hebrew and his choice to show the presentation of the Law echoes that Calvinist concept of the divine gift of the Ten Commandments with genuine sympathy. The artist only turns Jews into hostile caricatures in New Testament scenes that show them actively rejecting Jesus as the fulfilment of Old Testament prophecy (as in *John the Baptist Preaching* or the *Hundred-guilder Print*). Rembrandt also realized that the medieval Catholic tradition of showing Moses with horns stems from a Latin mistranslation by St Jerome of the Hebrew that describes 'rays' on his head after his contact with the Lord on Sinai. So his *Moses* instead shows curly locks that might appear horn-like, yet remain natural. Whether Moses holds up the tablets in anger to bring them crashing down in protest against the idolatry of the Golden Calf remains ambiguous, although his luminous face reveals little rage; Moses more readily seems to be displaying these commandments as the seal of the covenant and the true founding of the Jewish people. His brooding, serious face and the virtual monochrome brown palette of this broadly brushed late painting create a solemn mood for this frontal, life-sized figure.

Around the same moment the new Amsterdam City Hall commissioned for its Magistrates' Court a crowded narrative image of *Moses Descending from Mount Sinai* (completed in 1666; illus. 18) from Rembrandt's former pupil Ferdinand Bol. This alternate image further underscores the typological connection of the Dutch Calvinists to their biblical ancestors as well as the significance of Moses-as-lawgiver for that modern city-state.

Certainly Rembrandt images in paintings and prints often turned to the story of the Jewish patriarch Abraham,

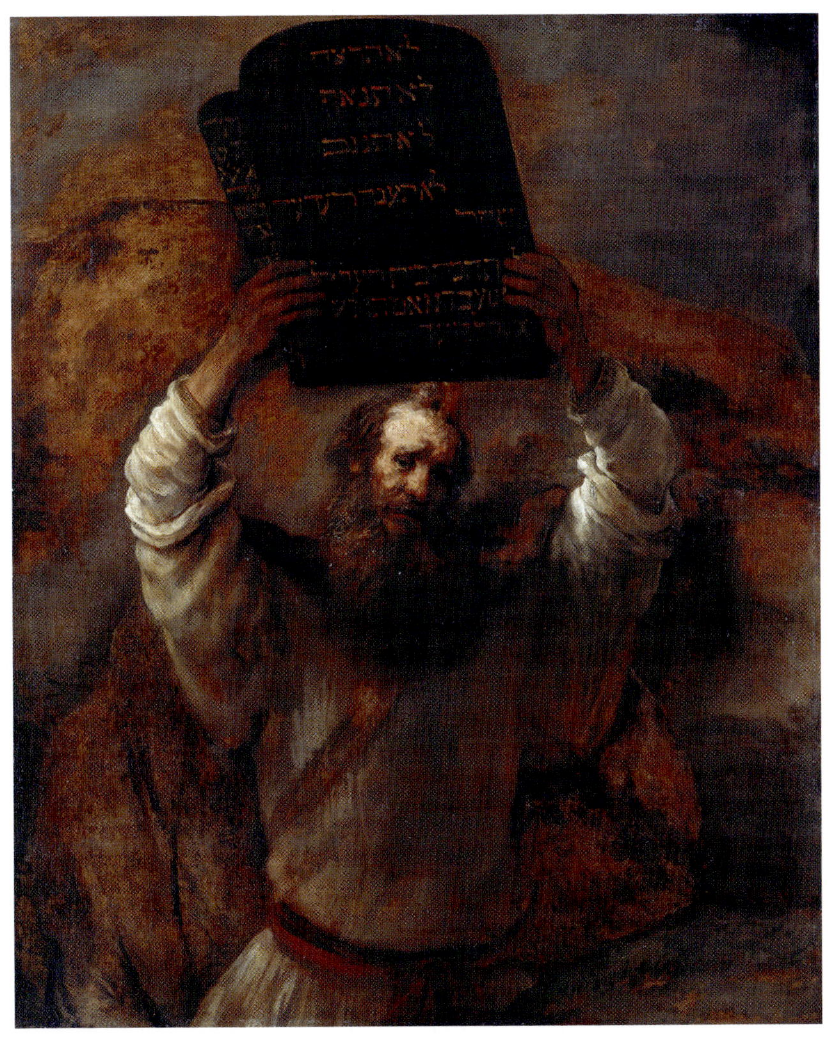

31 Rembrandt, *Moses with the Tablets of the Law*, 1659, oil on canvas.

founder of the religion and paragon of faithfulness. The key text of Abraham's obedience to God was his willingness to offer up his son and favourite Isaac as a human sacrifice in response to God's terrifying command (Genesis 22:1–19). Rembrandt depicted this harrowing scene on several occasions. A large and dramatic painting (1635) shows at full length the last-minute *deus ex machina* intervention of the angel, stopping Abraham's hand so suddenly that the knife is captured hovering in mid-air. A more reflective etching of 1645 (B. 34), by contrast, shows the dialogue between father and son prior to the climax, when the youthful Isaac, holding a faggot for the fire, asks about the missing animal to be sacrificed, and Abraham, dressed in a turban, points to heaven and replies (Genesis 22:7–8) that the Lord will provide. But Rembrandt's last word on the subject, an etching of 1655 (B. 35; illus. 32), combines both narrative elements within a new compassion for the relationship between God and man. While the dramatic moment still represents the climax of the scene, Abraham remains poised with his knife lifted above a kneeling Isaac, whose eyes he shields from his own actions as well as from the accompanying dark thoughts. But now, while stopping his deed with firm hands upon both Abraham's arms, the angel also firmly embraces the patriarch, enfolding him from behind. (Annotation in the *Statenbijbel* provides the prompt for this drama, noting that 'the angel came from behind'.) Although a divine light of visible rays bathes all the main figures in grace from above, Rembrandt has added one more feature to the spare text: he shows Abraham with eyes almost invisible in their deep, dark sockets. Again, the *Statenbijbel* commentary may guide the imagery, for it notes

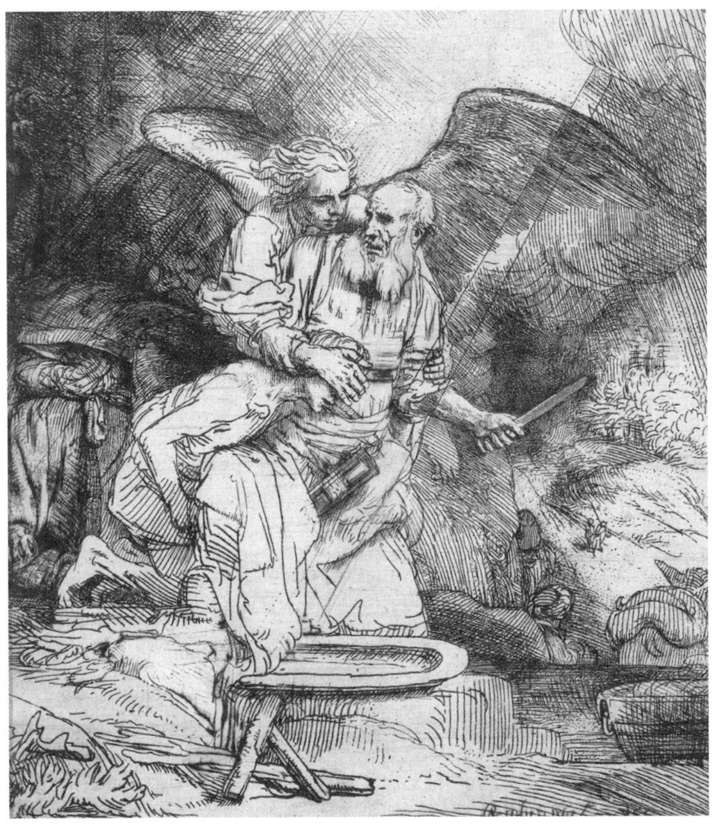

(Genesis 22:14) the importance of this moment of inner revelation in the name of the site, Mount Moriah, meaning 'sight or vision of God'.

Rembrandt has been justly celebrated, especially in his later works, for precisely this ability to focus on the inner reflections of individuals, particularly of biblical actors. Nowhere is this meditational stillness better deployed than in his *Bathsheba* (1654; illus. 33), where the protagonist, who will unintentionally tempt King David into adultery, but who

32 Rembrandt, *Sacrifice of Isaac*, 1655, etching.

will become the mother of his heir King Solomon (II Samuel II), is shown isolated except for a shadowy maidservant. The letter in her hand is the only indication of communication from David or suggestion of the narrative besides her foot-washing. Her physical beauty is obvious from her nude body, unselfconsciously presented to the viewer's gaze while lighted against a dark background, whereas her downcast head in profile and distracted gaze suggest that she is lost in conflicted thought between desire and marital fidelity.

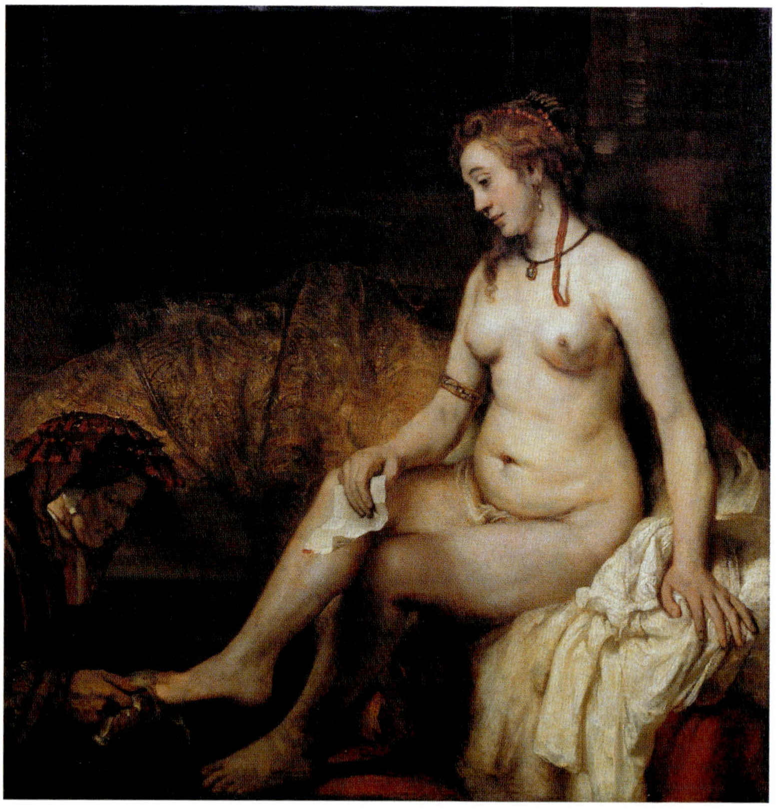

33 Rembrandt, *Bathsheba*, 1656, oil on canvas.

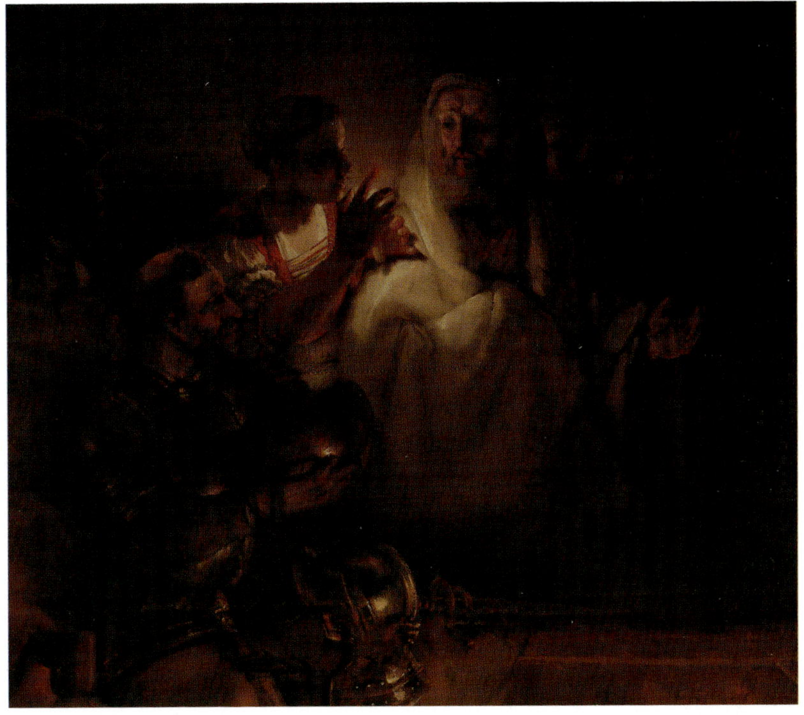

Of course, the painting of a full-length female nude also marks a summit of art for celebrated old masters admired by Rembrandt, notably Titian and Rubens. But this figure is so lifelike that many observers have wanted to see this figure as based on Rembrandt's common-law wife, Hendrickje Stoffels, rather than on some ideal. Indeed the date may also be significant, for Hendrickje was summoned in that very year to appear before Reformed Church officials for living in sin with the painter. While the scene of Bathsheba bathing and being observed by David from his palace was often used to epitomize the seductive power of women and the

34 Rembrandt, *Denial of Peter*, 1660, oil on canvas.

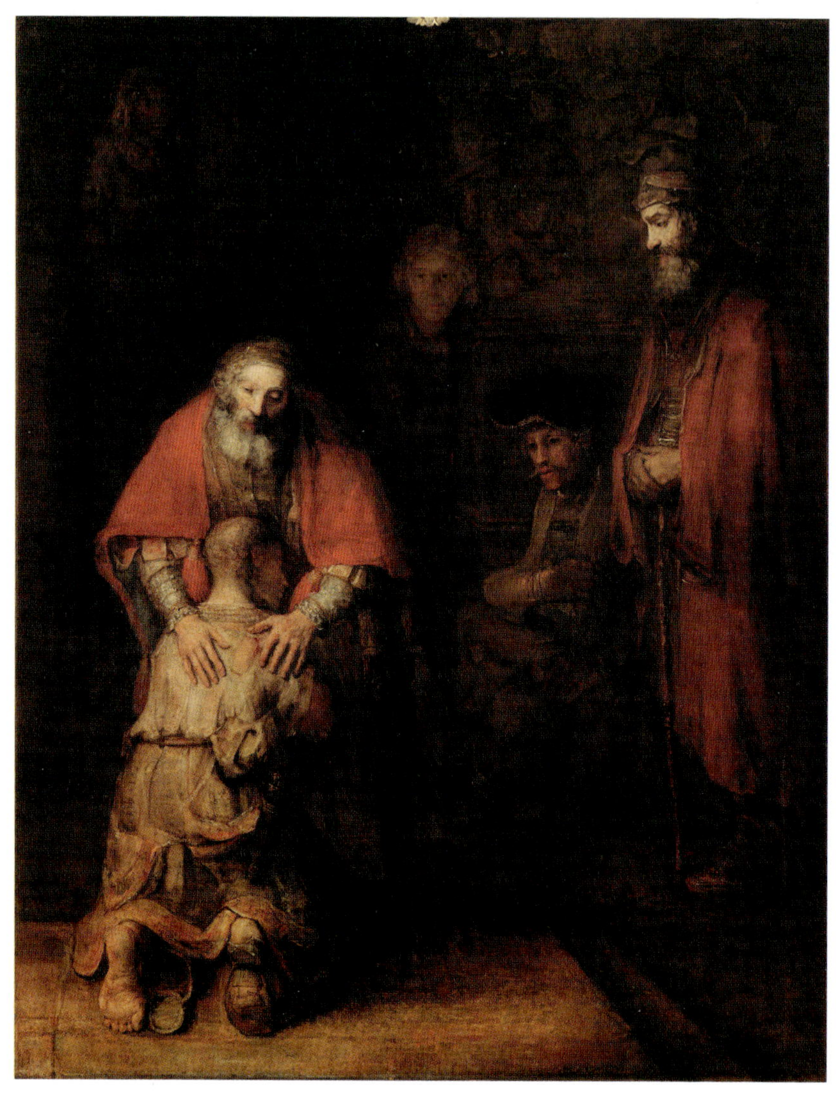

35 Rembrandt, *Return of the Prodigal Son*, c. 1668, oil on canvas.

breaking of the commandment against adultery, this woman is presented as a sympathetic, entirely human figure in both body and soul, just as the *Statenbijbel* presents her favourably, as 'converted to the true religion'.

Even saints in the New Testament can have their critical moments of doubt. The *Denial of Peter* (1660; illus. 34) uses close-up, half-length figures in the foreground to focus attention on an intimate encounter, the moment when the apostle, declared by Jesus to be the 'rock' ('petrus', Matthew 16:18) of his Church, nevertheless succumbs to self-preservation when he is threatened with recognition by the enemies of the Church (Luke 22:54–62). For the mysterious atmosphere of this nocturne, Rembrandt uses the device of the hidden candle, glowing beneath the hand of the maidservant who confronts Peter with discovery; this technique was a favourite feature of Utrecht artists from Rembrandt's youth during the 1620s, such as Gerrit van Honthorst and Hendrick ter Bruggen, both of whom depicted this same subject. Nearby the glow highlights metal surfaces on the armour of an observing and threatening foreground soldier, who underscores the menace of Peter's situation. The disciple himself hides beneath a head-covering that resembles a Jewish prayer-shawl (perhaps referring to his role as apostle to the Jews) and gestures his denial, just as Jesus had predicted; in the right background shadows, Jesus is being led away to his Passion torments, but he turns towards Peter as if to acknowledge that the prophecy has come true. The passage concludes that Peter wept bitterly, a scene that the young Rembrandt had already meticulously depicted at full length and in isolation: *St Peter in Prison* (1631), where the nearby keys identify the white-bearded apostle with clasped hands. By contrast, the late Amsterdam picture is broadly brushed in thick paint, with manipulated contrasts of brightness and clarity. But the lasting effect is the complex pantomime of conflicted emotions on the face of the vacillating saint.

Rembrandt's overall emphasis in his late narrative images remains on the human figure in a serious mood – sometimes both serious and biblical, as in the moral dilemmas he presented in his versions of *Bathsheba* or *Denial of Peter*. He has given up his earlier emphasis on dramatic, gestural action and close description in favour of evocative dark, moody lighting and quiet, still isolation.

In one of his very last paintings, possibly uncompleted at his death, Rembrandt returns to the preached words of Jesus for his subject: the parable (Luke 15:11–32) of the Return of the Prodigal Son (illus. 35). This is a story of repentance, where 'there will be more joy in heaven over one sinner who repents.' The depicted moment shows the contrition and absolute submission of the wayward son who squandered his patrimony and returned humiliated and in rags to his father, only to be reconciled and received home unconditionally and with a great feast of rejoicing. Rembrandt once again had depicted the same scene earlier, in an etching (1636; B. 91), where the active family drama appears in profile on the home steps. By contrast, the late painting, over life-sized, shows only the two main figures with the son's head lost in shadow, enfolded in the welcoming arms of his father, in a gesture more like a benediction than an embrace, staged before a threshold. In warm gold and red colours that glow against a dark background, punctuated only by silent, standing observer figures, an aged Rembrandt conveys the timeless Christian message that true repentance of sins and obedient submission will be rewarded with unmerited grace from a heavenly Father. He who once was lost now is found (Luke 15:32).

THREE

Rembrandt and the Orange Court

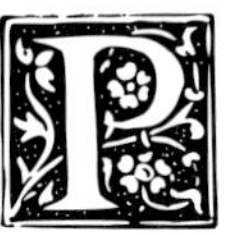ETER RAUL RUBENS (1577–1640) was a court artist of international standing. He was raised at court by a father who served as legal counsellor to the wife of William the Silent, and his first main position was as court painter to the Gonzagas in Mantua (from 1600 to 1608). He made diplomatic trips throughout his career and even used his skills as a painter to further peace efforts by his local monarchs, the regents Albert and Isabella in Brussels, who appointed him their court painter on his return to Antwerp in 1609. He was ennobled by the king of Spain in 1624, even while he worked on a major panegyric cycle for Marie de' Medici, queen mother of France. After a visit to Spain in 1628, he was sent on as emissary of that crown to England (from 1629 to 1630), where Charles I knighted him at Whitehall (whose ceiling decorations for Banqueting House he would send back from Antwerp in 1636). He met Frederik Hendrik in The Hague in 1631 and was reappointed court painter by his new regent, Cardinal-Infante Ferdinand, before embarking on his last great painting cycle, the mythological pictures for the Spanish royal hunting lodge, the Torre de la Parada. Rubens also consorted regularly with aristocrats, diplomats and collectors, many of whose duties overlapped.

Thus Rubens remained an enduring role model for a younger Rembrandt and many other artists in the Dutch-speaking world, where political and religious divisions did not preclude considering the Flemish master as one of their own. That internationalism and praise from the North Netherlands emerges clearly from the autobiography (written 1629–31) of Constantijn Huygens, who called Rubens the 'Apelles of our time' in echo of the privileged relationship between that legendary classical Greek painter and his patron Alexander the Great. He praises Rubens for diplomacy as well as painting, and for his knowledge in all fields, but singles out one picture in particular, a *Medusa*, for praise in its combination of horror with charm.

Like Rubens, Huygens was born to a life at court; his father was secretary to William the Silent, and in 1625 he in turn became the indispensable secretary to stadholder Frederik Hendrik (1584–1647) in The Hague, serving three stadholders of the House of Orange. He too was knighted in England for his service at the Court of St James. His duties involved frequent literary contact with Huygens, who was also an accomplished musician and a sophisticated author in his own right, who even translated poems by John Donne into Dutch. Huygens, a connoisseur of contemporary Dutch painters, had his likeness painted by several artists, including Jan Lievens (1628) as well as numerous others. (One scholar, Eric Jan Sluijter, asserts that 'It would be difficult to find another seventeenth-century Dutch person who had his portrait painted more often.')

Constantijn Huygens with His Clerk (1627; illus. 36) by Thomas de Keyser, Amsterdam's leading portraitist before Rembrandt, shows him at full length but seated, busy receiving a message at his desk, covered with a rich carpet. In his well-furnished study, a classical mantelpiece with painting and a hanging figural tapestry with his own coat of arms together present a suggestion of wealth and status. Huygens sports a single glove, a privilege of noblemen, and poses in costume finery, although worn as a wool riding suit. In deference his clerk has removed his own hat while Huygens retains his. But the secretary also parades his knowledge, showing a compass on his desk as he works on plans for architecture (possibly for one of the stadholder's new palaces), plus a pair of celestial and terrestrial globes nearby (his son Christiaan became a famous scientist with international connections), and a lute-like instrument. Pen and ink and books attest to his correspondence as well as his literary activity. Thus, as revealed in this sensitive portrait, Huygens set a sophisticated, cosmopolitan tone for the court of his Orange stadholder in The Hague, and his De Keyser portrait reveals him as an elegant courtly practitioner of both serious state business (*negotium*) and aristocratic leisure (*otium*), in accordance with a learned classical ideal going back to Cicero.

That international flavour was reinforced by the presence, after the outbreak of the Thirty Years War, of Frederick v, the 'Winter King', Elector Palatine and briefly Protestant king of Bohemia (from 1619 to 1620) before he was deposed after the Battle of White Mountain, sparking intensified pan-European religious conflict. As a leader of the Protestant allies in Central Europe, after 1621 he found refuge for a decade of lavish exile with his princess bride Elizabeth (d. 1661), daughter of James 1 of England, at the court of his uncle, stadholder

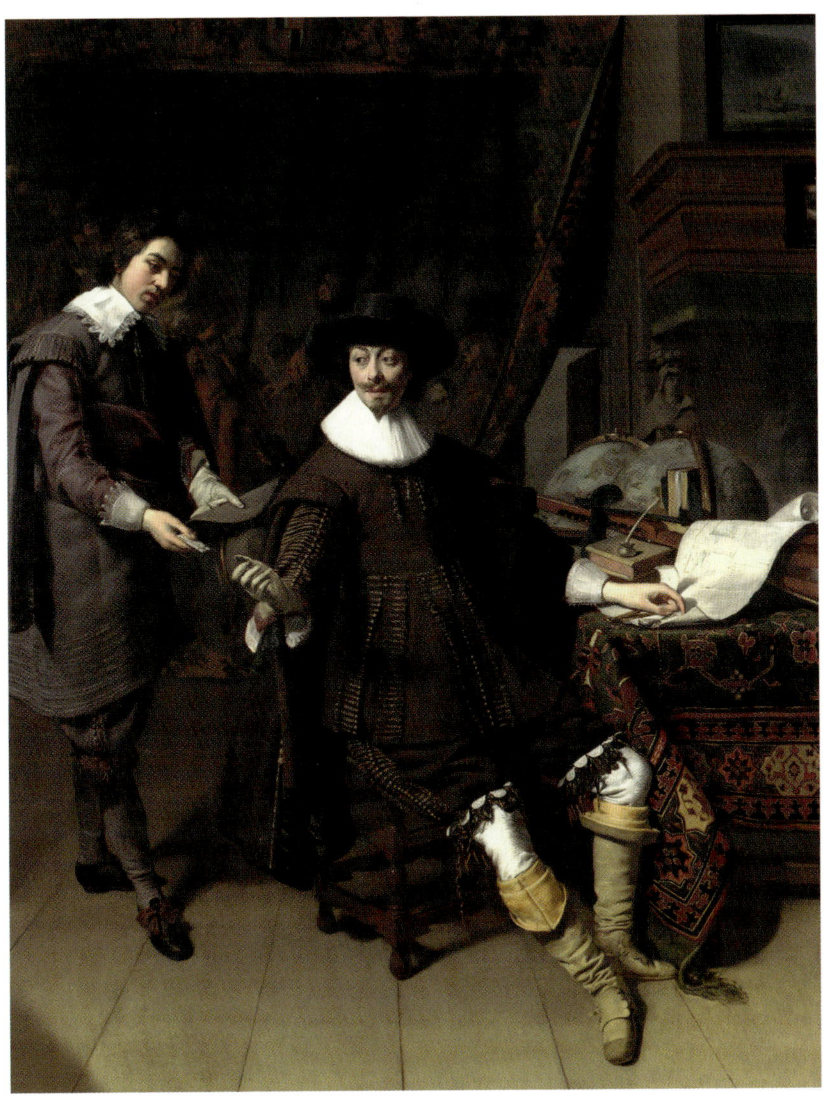

36 Thomas de Keyser, *Constantijn Huygens with His Clerk*, 1627, oil on panel.

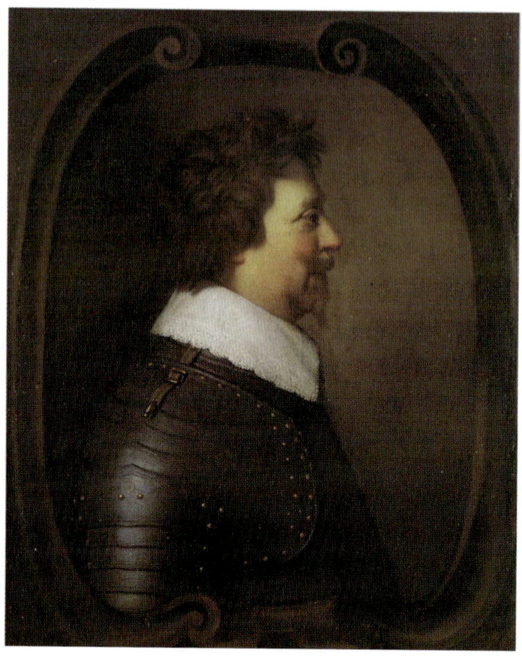

Maurits. Their portraits by such leading court portraitists as Gerrit van Honthorst record their Bohemian court-within-a-court at The Hague. Anthony van Dyck (1599–1641), who visited The Hague in the winter of 1631/2, also painted superb full-length portraits of Prince Charles Louis and Prince Rupert, the two oldest surviving sons of Frederick and Elizabeth, both in The Hague and later when they visited their cousins at the English court after 1635, in a double portrait in armour with baton and military order (1637).

Van Dyck, the acknowledged master of the stylish court portrait, also painted an earlier, striking half-length of Frederik Hendrik in military armour standing with his baton of command before a fortress-like rusticated wall (*c.* 1628–9). The

37 Gerrit van Honthorst, *Frederik Hendrik*, 1631, oil on canvas.

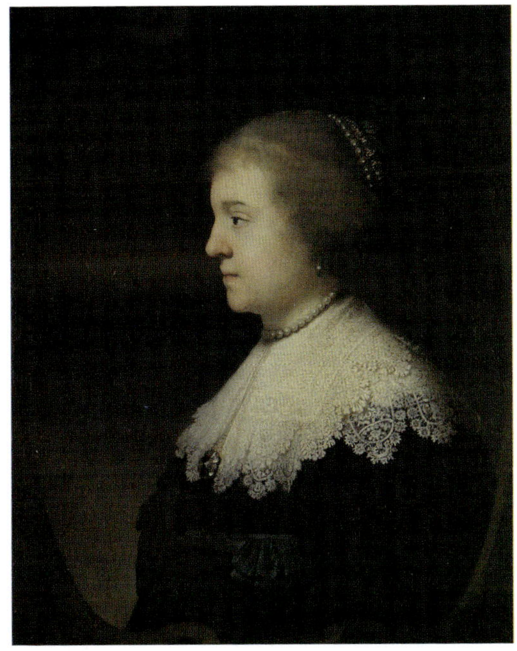

basic composition depends on a well-established convention for monarchs and commanders established by Titian during the previous century and already imitated by Dutch portraitists of Frederik Hendrik, particularly Michiel van Miereveld in a full-length, standing portrait. Van Dyck's companion portrait of Frederik's consort, Amalia van Solms, shows her seated in an armchair, her body angled to face the stadholder pendant, her face turned to the viewer.

Such was the court environment in The Hague to which Rembrandt aspired. He even took the opportunity to produce a profile portrait of Amalia van Solms (1632; illus. 38) as a complement to the profile of Frederik Hendrik painted by Gerrit van Honthorst (1631; illus. 37). Honthorst (1592–1656)

38 Rembrandt, *Amalia van Solms*, 1632, oil on canvas.

stemmed from Utrecht and made a name for himself with genre and religious paintings with strong chiaroscuro effects derived from Caravaggio's model in Rome, which he visited from around 1613 to 1620. Rubens visited his studio in 1627. But then Honthorst also spent time at the court of Charles I in London in 1628, where he made portraits of the monarchs and painted a masque-like allegory, where the Duke of Buckingham as Mercury leads the Liberal Arts to Charles I as Apollo and his queen Henrietta Maria as Diana. Honthorst even executed a monumental commission from Christian IV of Denmark on Danish history for Kronborg Castle between 1635 and 1639, although he remained based in The Hague, where he worked for the Winter King.

Rembrandt used the same kind of interior oval frame with scrollwork for Amalia as Honthorst had used for the stad-holder. He again wears armour with a lace collar, akin to her richer lace and pearl choker. However, a 1632 inventory reveals that her portrait already hung alone, suggesting that it did not find favour with her; it might also have been both more literal and less flattering than the prevailing airbrushed softness of Van Dyck, or even of Honthorst himself, who soon produced his own profile pendant, probably to replace that of Rembrandt (illus. 39; undated). Amalia in Rembrandt's portrait (still signed RHL, with his Leiden affiliation) shows a slight double chin, frizzy hair and a kind of square-jawed piety. Huygens also seems to have frowned on another Rembrandt portrait of the period, claiming in a Latin distich of 1633 that the portrait of his friend Jacques de Gheyn III, which ends with the line,

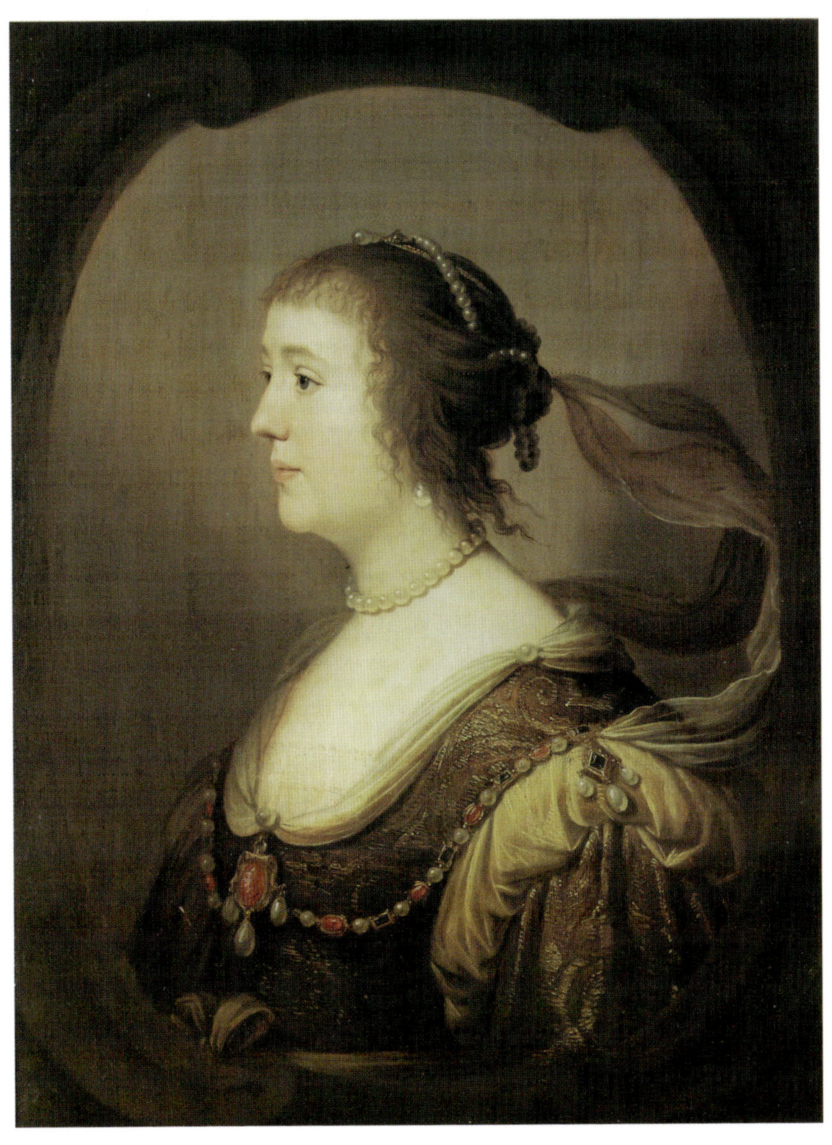

39 Gerrit van Honsthorst, *Amalia van Solms*, 1630s, oil on panel.

> The hand is that of Rembrandt, the features are de
>   Gheyn's.
> Admire it, reader, though it's not de Gheyn at all.

Thereafter, despite all the other portraits commissioned by Huygens, he never asked Rembrandt, already Amsterdam's most gifted and popular portraitist, to make another one.

Still, Rembrandt as well as Lievens had already been singled out, even as young painters, by the influential Huygens, who devotes quite a section of his memoirs to these two promising young painters, 'miracles of talent and skill', despite their modest backgrounds. He claims that Rembrandt surpasses Lievens in bringing out the essence of his subjects, often with a sure touch in a smaller format, and he particularly singles out the gesture of the repentant title figure from the 1629 *Judas Returning the Thirty Pieces of Silver*. Lievens is praised for his portraits and for his audacious, large-scale forms. Huygens cautions them both for their cockiness and recommends that they visit Italy, like Rubens and Honthorst.

Around 1632 Huygens went on to commission from Rembrandt a series of paintings on the Passion of Christ (see the *Descent from the Cross*; illus. 27). Emulating the works of Rubens, so esteemed by Huygens and the stadholder, which Rembrandt would have known from engraved reproductions, he nevertheless made the imagery far more painfully human than Rubens's spiritual sublime. Rembrandt also provided a strong personal and emotional connection to the scenes by inserting his own self-portrait, as a tormentor in the *Raising of the Cross* and as a compassionate follower in the *Descent from the Cross*.

In 1636 Rembrandt wrote to Huygens that he was working on three further paintings in the same format as part of the commission on the Passion for Frederik Hendrik: an Entombment, a Resurrection and an Ascension (all 1636), sent in that year. A third letter appeared only in 1639, when the latter two paintings were finally delivered. In that letter Rembrandt declares uniquely that his goal is to convey the 'greatest and most natural e/motion [*beweechgelickheyt*]'. The artist also curried favour by sending Huygens a gift of his own, a large piece 'ten feet long and eight feet high' (which has been identified with the large *Blinding of Samson*, Frankfurt; see below). A later letter of 1639 asks for a considerable fee increase, 'not less than a thousand guilders' each for the two most recent pictures – suggesting that Rembrandt's influence with Huygens and, indirectly, with the stadholder was beginning to fray. To complete the story: one year before Frederik Hendrik died, he paid Rembrandt 2,400 guilders for two works from the Infancy of Christ rather than the Passion – an *Adoration of the Shepherds* (1646) and a *Circumcision* (lost) – but there is no further evidence of contact between Rembrandt and either Huygens or the stadholder.

It is perhaps worth noting that, despite his initial openness toward the Arminian or Remonstrant religious faction, in part by not enforcing the bans on their prayer gatherings, that degree of religious toleration was short lived. In 1633 – the year in which Rembrandt's first two Passion paintings were sent to The Hague – the stadholder firmly sided with the war party and their fellow-travellers, the Counter-Remonstrants. His move towards greater authority and centralization thus was accompanied by a shift in religious sympathies and perhaps a much-reduced interest in religious art under the influence of orthodox Calvinists. In 1635 Frederik Hendrik even denied Rubens access to the country at a time of increased military alliance with France against Catholic Spain and the South Netherlands out of his concern for a negotiated peace. Moreover, the ruler also was investing much more heavily in his own surroundings, especially the ambitious retreat of Honselaersdijk (completed 1638) as well as ter Nieuburg at Rijswijk (1634–8) and the residence of Noordeinde in The Hague. Gardens and costly tapestries (designed by Honthorst) comprised the major artistic expenditures.

The likeliest candidate for the large canvas, ten by eight feet (2.05 × 2.72m), which Rembrandt wished to send to Huygens in 1639, is his horrific *Blinding of Samson* (1636; illus. 40), a work that was calculated to appeal to the admirer of Rubens's *Medusa*. This Old Testament biblical scene (Judges 16:19–21) is the climax of the betrayal of the heroic strongman, whose strength had come from his unshorn hair, still visible in the vestiges of his thick beard. The temptress Delilah appears in the top centre of the picture, racing away with scissors in hand while holding the clipped tresses of Samson; she stares, wild-eyed, backwards and downwards at the consequences of her conspiracy. There a crowd of four armed Philistines pinion the arms of the strongman, while one of them brutally stabs him in the eye to blind him, and blood visibly spurts out. Rembrandt has pulled out all the stops in this rendering, featuring strong chiaroscuro that silhouettes one of the attackers against the backlighting at the mouth of the tent, reinforced by meticulously rendered glints of light reflecting off armour, chains and even a golden ewer at the left edge of the canvas. That vessel and the luxurious carpet on the floor suggest earlier luxurious indulgence, enhanced by alcohol.

Most of these features – dynamic action with broad gestures and careful attention to pictorial details of light and texture – appeared in the near-contemporary *Belshazzar's Feast* (see illus. 28), another large, early biblical subject, so Rembrandt might well have been advertising his most current range of skills to Huygens, his early admirer and potential advocate at court. His massive hero seems also to echo the work of Rubens, such as his heroic, writhing, nude *Prometheus* (*c.* 1611–12), based in turn on the study of ancient sculpture, especially the *Laocoön* in Rome, but again Rembrandt presents a distinctly more ordinary body, bulky rather than muscled,

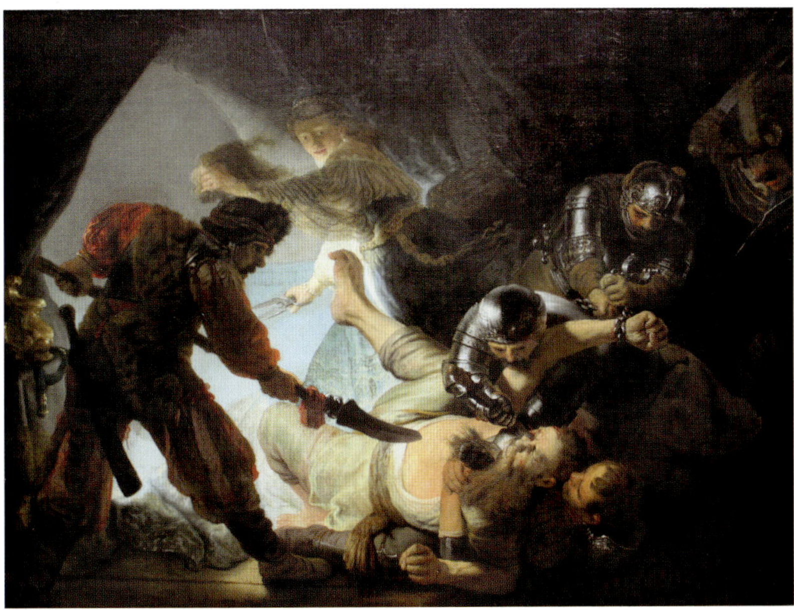

40 Rembrandt, *Blinding of Samson*, 1636, oil on canvas.

and a face with coarse features. Again the indirect influence of Caravaggio might have heightened this quotidian aspect of the hero as well as the physicality of the gruesome pain and suffering, conveyed by the hero through his clenched teeth, fists and even toes, visible just below Delilah. Rembrandt surely wished to emphasize this horror as well as his attention to lighting and details; his 1639 letter to Huygens advises the recipient to 'hang this piece in a strong light and in such a way that one can stand far back, then it will sparkle well'.

In another large painting that might have held particular meaning for a sophisticated viewer, Rembrandt twisted the conventional viewing of *Ganymede* (1635; illus. 41). Usually this myth (Ovid, *Metamorphoses* 10:155ff.) allows an artist to show a beautiful Trojan youth snatched by the eagle of Jupiter to be borne up to Olympus and serve as cupbearer of the gods, and such images by Rubens and major Italian Renaissance artists prevailed for the subject. However, because Christian interpreters of this pagan myth most often likened it to the raptures of divine love for the soul and deliberately over-looked its more obvious homosexual eroticism, another option was to show the young Ganymede as a charming cherub, like the images in contemporary emblem books about love. Rembrandt himself even painted a 1634 *Cupid Blowing a Soap Bubble* (reproduced as an etching by Jan Van Vliet), which combines a *vanitas* motif of evanescence with the mythical youthful archer of love, akin to the emblems of Daniel Heinsius (*Bulla favor*, 'favour is a bubble'). Karel van Mander's 1604 Dutch reading of Ovid emphasizes that Ganymede 'represents the human soul that is least defiled by the bodily impurity of depraved lusts'. But Van Mander goes on to assert

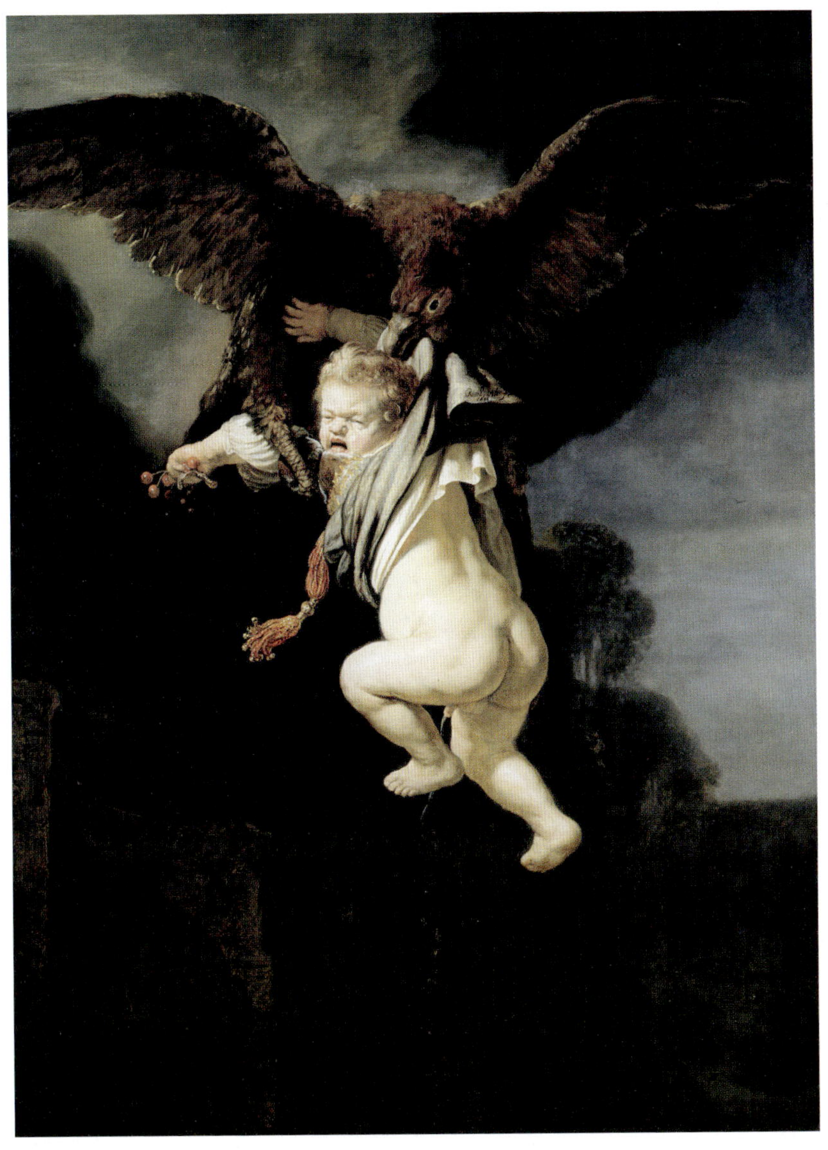

41 Rembrandt, *Ganymede*, 1635, oil on canvas.

that Ganymede was later transformed into the constellation Aquarius, which might be signalled by his outpouring liquid, and some interpreters have followed that line, seeing the painting as having a learned dimension, despite the unruly behaviour it depicts.

Rembrandt, however, instead of merely transforming the ephebe into a cherub, has further debased his behaviour by showing him as a mewling infant who pisses in fright as he is lifted aloft by the large bird, itself more like a vulture than a heroic eagle, akin to the bird by Rubens that torments *Prometheus* (as painted by animal specialist Frans Snyders). Here, too, Rembrandt might have had a particular recent Netherlandish model in mind – the celebrated sculpture Manneken Pis by Jérôme Duquesnoy in Brussels – but as usual he undercuts even its bold decorum and attractiveness with the quotidian howling cries, pissing reaction and exposed bottom of the chubby infant. Moreover, in portraits that conflated children with Ganymede, such as those made by Rembrandt's own pupil Nicolaes Maes in the 1670s, all the children depicted are babies (for example, *George de Vicq as Ganymede*).

Rembrandt made a rare preparatory study (Dresden) for the painted figure, and in those same years he also busied himself in both finished drawings (*c.* 1635; *The Naughty Boy*) and etchings (1635; *Pancake Woman*, B. 124) with carefully studied images of active, even squirming infants. It should also be noted that Rembrandt showed little embarrassment in depicting body functions in such etchings as his *Man Pissing* (B. 190) and *Woman Pissing* (B. 191), both dated to 1631. (This act is fairly commonly placed at the margins of earlier scenes of festivity, such as Pieter Bruegel images of peasants dancing, emulated in turn by Rubens in his *Kermis, c.* 1635–8 [Paris].)

The large size and low viewpoint of *Ganymede* suggest, however, that it was destined for placement over a mantel in a large living room, suggesting that this image is not merely a parody of the decorous presentation that usually surrounds mythological imagery. The theme even provided decoration for ceiling paintings, including the lantern vault of the stadholder's palace at Honselaersdijk (commissioned 1638, probably by Pieter de Grebber; noted in 1640 by English diarist John Evelyn) and the later vault of the Oranjezaal at the Huis ten Bosch by Honthorst – painted in conjunction with an image of the *Marriage of Frederik Hendrik with Amalia van Solms*, where clearly the message of the myth signifies divine love. That Rembrandt's infant carries cherries in his hand could accord with the presence of such fruit in religious paintings, signifying the joys of heaven, but this painting defies any ready interpretation identifying Ganymede with divine love. More likely is the reading that sees the cherries, like grape stems in some family portraits, as the indication of the (literally) fruitful succession of an heir to the family.

Most recently, Barbara Gaeghtens (in an unpublished lecture) has proposed insightfully that Rembrandt's *Ganymede* might be invoking yet another ancient myth regarding rulers – that they submit to an 'eagle test', where their strength and courage could be measured by hauling them into the air and towards the bright sun on the wings of an eagle to test their mettle. Other depictions of a younger Ganymede show the infant riding on the back of the eagle, rather than the youth who is upraised by the raptor. Clearly Rembrandt's infant, hauled involuntarily upward by the great bird and howling in fright and pissing, is abjectly failing his eagle test. And the otherwise unexplained tasselled cord around his chemise, now tugged upwards by the eagle, would echo the sash of command worn by generals in the field, but also by princes as their status prerogative as commanders-in-chief (compare the state portraits of stadholder Maurits of Nassau, wearing armour and the same coloured sash; Michiel van Miereveld; *c.* 1625). Now, however, that very status-marker hangs in useless irony, undercut by the obvious terror of the vulnerable baby. In terms of timing, if this painting refers to the young prince of the Netherlands, the stadholder's son William II (b. 1626), then he would be considerably older than the infant of the painting. But young Willem II featured in the new Orange dynastic strategy of conferring ruling succession in advance, including his advantageous marital alliance (to Mary Stuart, daughter of the English king, Charles I, in 1641). His sudden death in 1650 would inaugurate a precarious 'stadholderless' period in the Netherlands. Possibly Rembrandt's *Ganymede* as a failed eagle test could be indirectly criticizing that young heir to the title of stadholder, then ten years old, in contrast to more celebratory portraits: as a toddler in long skirts by van Dyck (*c.* 1631); as a teen in Roman armour by Honthorst (1640); and the double portrait on the occasion of his wedding (1641), also by van Dyck. If that veiled criticism is correct, Rembrandt was painting *Ganymede* as an insider image for a sophisticated, prominent viewer, presumably an Amsterdam patrician with a more liberal outlook, opposed to the hardening factions between court and city.

Another pictorial record of a growing ambivalence toward the court by Rembrandt is his small sketch, presumably a *modello* for a political print that was never issued, called the *Concord of the State* (*c.* 1640; illus. 42), a work that was still in Rembrandt's personal collection when it was inventoried for bankruptcy in 1656. This is a dense allegory, filled with old-fashioned military figures, many of them armoured and on horseback, who surround a chained lion resting on a bundle of shafts, presumably the *Leo Belgicus*, the symbol of a once united and militant Netherlands on early maps. What makes the image difficult to interpret is the question of whether it represents an ideal political situation or an editorial on the current state of Dutch politics. Still further complications emerge regarding its date of origin; a strip at the bottom right with the signature and date is inconclusive: 'Rembrandt.f.

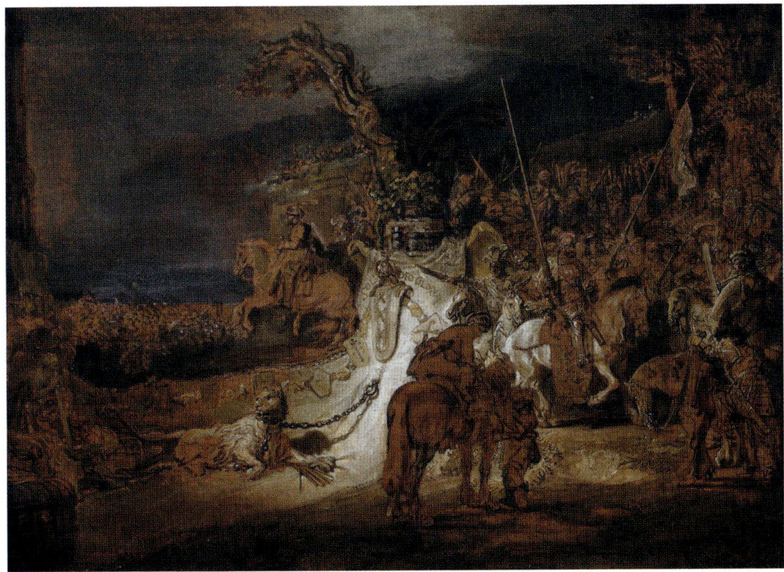

42 Rembrandt, *The Concord of the State*, *c.* 1640, oil on panel.

164–'. By the late 1630s the Dutch campaigns against the Spanish in their territories were going well; the Spanish hold on Breda of 1625 (celebrated a decade later in Velázquez's famous painting of the Dutch surrender for the Madrid Buen Retiro Palace) had been broken, and the city was recaptured by the Dutch in 1637. Nevertheless, major Dutch cities, led by Amsterdam, resisted the high war expenditures and favoured free trade, so they conflicted with Frederik Hendrik and the war party.

The shackled lion in Dutch propaganda clearly symbolizes the subjugation of the would-be Netherlands nation. It is shorn of its mane, usually typical of the Belgian Lion figure, so weakened, like Samson, of its strength and ferocity. The bundle of shafts on which it rests signifies the United Provinces as a group, under its protection, but not bound together in strength like a *fasces* bundle. At the left horizon a hostile army appears under a menacing sky. At the left edge, however, a tall column, on which hangs a document with five seals, provides steadfast support and suggests the Union of Utrecht of 1579, which founded the eventual Dutch Republic with five provinces. Beneath it, treasure chests denote prosperity, at risk under the attack. The blindfolded figure of Justice leans on her sword behind an empty throne in this corner, from which one of the chains for the lion emerges. Linked coats of arms behind the lion culminate in a larger heraldic shield with the triple-X city seal of Amsterdam, and Haarlem and Leiden arms are also visible nearby, as a brilliant light falls on that centre, accompanied by the Latin inscription 'all glory to God' (*Soli deo gloria*). Thus the common good under divine protection is invoked in the cause of national survival at a moment of peril. Atop the hill a blasted tree stands, but it has a renewing green shoot at its base.

Their defence is uncertain. Most of the soldiers assemble to the right of the bright hillock with the Amsterdam coat of arms; their dense numbers before the right horizon feature pikes and muskets like the *Nightwatch* militia company portrait of 1642. They are led by an armoured knight on horseback with a lance in the right foreground, a throwback to late medieval warfare, and by a second figure hoisting a banner behind him. Another lone mounted knight, separated from the main force, advances towards the enemy from above the lion, rearing his horse in a stately levade that remained a standard in equestrian portraits across the century.

To identify these commanders with too much specificity defeats the allegorical imagery of the picture. Indeed, the very ambiguity of the picture suggests a deliberate obscurity by the painter. The united cities can be seen either as the essential core of the United Provinces or as their implacable sources of disorder. The military, by contrast, can also be seen in two ways – either as riding to the rescue of the nation or else as an archaic institution with obsolete, incapable leaders unfit for modern conditions, like the urban militia companies that had outlived their usefulness. Even the tree is ambiguous. As a symbol of the House of Orange, it can be read as exhausted or as renewed by the heir. Depending on when the picture actually dates, the controversy between city and court, between peace factions and war parties, and whether there was still ongoing support for Dutch participation in the seemingly endless Eighty Years War (now part of the Europe-wide Thirty Years War), must remain moot. Like most interpreters, Bram Kempers reads this image as support for the stadholder and the court, then allied with France, in which case Rembrandt could be seen as making a last-ditch effort to secure court patronage with an expression of sympathy for the need for a military defence of the cities and the nation as a whole. But Kempers also acknowledges that the image portrays Dutch society 'as a divided, post-feudal society and not the peaceful early modern bourgeois world of ministers and merchants', even as he sees the *Concord* image as a call for unity. Even the title, *The Concord of the Land*, recorded as part of the on-site 1656 inventory (as no. 106, located in the back room or *sael*, salon), could be understood ironically, underscoring the deep political divisions concerning the war, especially in Amsterdam, the city of Rembrandt, whose arms are so prominently featured beneath that blasted Orange trunk. But it could also be a call to arms of a positive kind, to rally the troops who form such an important portion of the imagery.

Much of the court construction so passionately pursued by Frederik Hendrik and supervised by Huygens has disappeared with time. But the main design force behind his constructions was a painter-architect, Jacob van Campen (1595–1657), who also designed Huygens's own house (1633; lost). The best way to judge how Van Campen adapted the latest Italianate architectural vocabulary can be seen in the elegant town house in The Hague, built for the cousin of the Orange stadholder, Prince Johan Maurits of Nassau-Siegen, regent for the nation during its brief possession (from 1637 to 1644) of the colony of Brazil. That house (today a major museum of Dutch art) is still known as the Mauritshuis

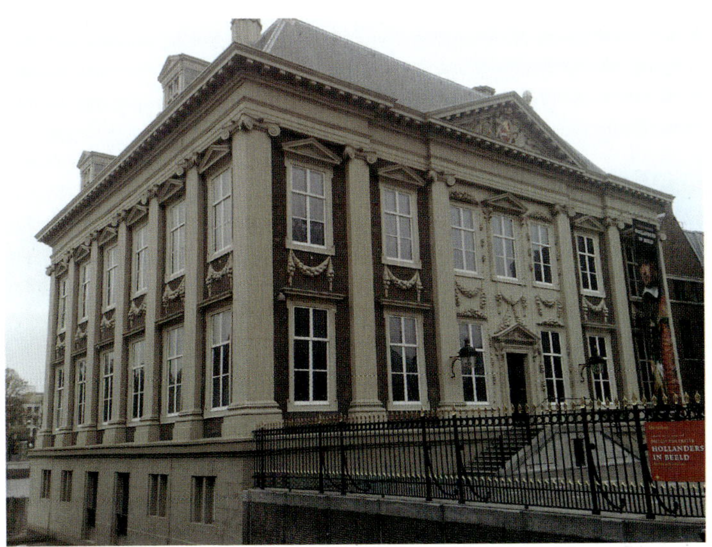

(illus. 43). Located at the corner of the Hofvijfer ('court pond') alongside the historic Dutch parliament (Binnenhof), it stood like a cornerstone alongside the nerve centre of the Orange court of the stadholder.

Its elegant proportions and colossal Ionic pilasters, resting on an articulated basement, emphasize the cubic exterior profile of the Mauritshuis. Its steep hipped roof echoes contemporary French architecture, whose classicism appears especially on the facade, crowned with a pediment. The interior was laid out in geometrical symmetry around a central grand staircase, in accord with published designs of Italian villas by Andrea Palladio (1570) and Vincenzo Scamozzi (1615) and probably also Rubens's 1622 book, *The Palaces of Genoa*. A tall central room upstairs had an arched ceiling, pierced by an innovative open square cupola, derived from Italian models and adopted in seventeenth-century France

43 Jacob van Campen and Pieter Post, Mauritshuis, The Hague, 1633–44.

(however, a disastrous fire in 1704 destroyed most of the house contents and altered some of its layout). In effect Van Campen's cupola design replaced the illusionistically open palace ceilings with figures such as musicians viewed from below, as painted by Honthorst (1622). In all likelihood that space originally housed the paintings and objects of Johan Maurits, the *Kunst- und Wunderkammer* that he brought back from Brazil.

If Rembrandt was losing his favour with Huygens and the stadholder by the end of the 1630s, the developments at court a decade later make clear just how far he stood from their increasingly classical taste. The major new commission in The Hague called for a dedicated building, the Huis ten Bosch (House in the Woods), a 'suburban villa' begun in 1645 for Amalia van Solms by Pieter Post, Van Campen's chief assistant in The Hague at the Mauritshuis, Noordeinde Palace and even the later Amsterdam Town Hall. Its design is simple: a brick building with a large cruciform domed hall at its centre. Again, models stem from Italy, for both the cruciform central space and the octagonal dome at its peak. The main room is decorated with a full suite of painted panegyrics in memory of Frederik Hendrik (d. 1647) – including works painted by Van Campen himself, who supervised these decorations. That great hall of the Huis ten Bosch, the Oranjezaal, was assigned to a variety of painters led by Jacob Jordaens, the principal Antwerp artist after the death of Rubens in 1640, and other Flemish followers of Rubens (Theodoor van Thulden, Pieter Soutman and Thomas Willeboirts Bosschaert). Nine Dutch artists also received lesser commissions.

The Oranjezaal subjects for the most part feature myth-ological figures, invoked as positive allegories on behalf of the stadholder's role as governor. Beside Van Campen's imagery (*Apollo and Aurora*; *Frederik Hendrik as Warrior on Horseback*), they were led by Cesar Boëtius van Everdingen (*Four Muses and Pegasus*; *Birth of Frederik Hendrik*; *Allegory on Marriage with Olympian Gods and Ganymede*) as well as by leading classicists from Haarlem, Pieter de Grebber (*The Apotheosis of Frederik Hendrik*) and Salomon de Bray (*Triumphal Arches*). Leading court favourite Honthorst painted scenes that emphasized portraits: *Marriage of Frederik Hendrik and Amalia van Solms*; *Steadfastness of Frederik Hendrik*; and *Amalia van Solms and Her Daughters*, presented as side observers to the basic theme of triumphal entry. A lesser assignment went to Huygens's former favourite Jan Lievens (*Five Muses*, complementing Everdingen), now painting in a far more Flemish classical manner. Rembrandt, by contrast, was conspicuously excluded from the Oranjezaal.

Jordaens, who also painted a *Triumph of Time* for the room, held pride of place there with his massive central image, around which all the other painted decorations revolved, particularly those with side images of observers under arches: *The Triumph of Frederik Hendrik* (signed and dated 1652). In preparation for this major commission Jordaens prepared a series of oil sketches, like Rubens, for the approval of his patrons as well as for his studio assistants, but also for Van Campen to co-ordinate with the other artists involved in the interior decorative layout. Closest to the final, grand-scale Oranjezaal composition is the large *modello* (1651; illus. 44), sent to Huygens along with a letter discussing its iconography. Two other sketches have been preserved. Jordaens also

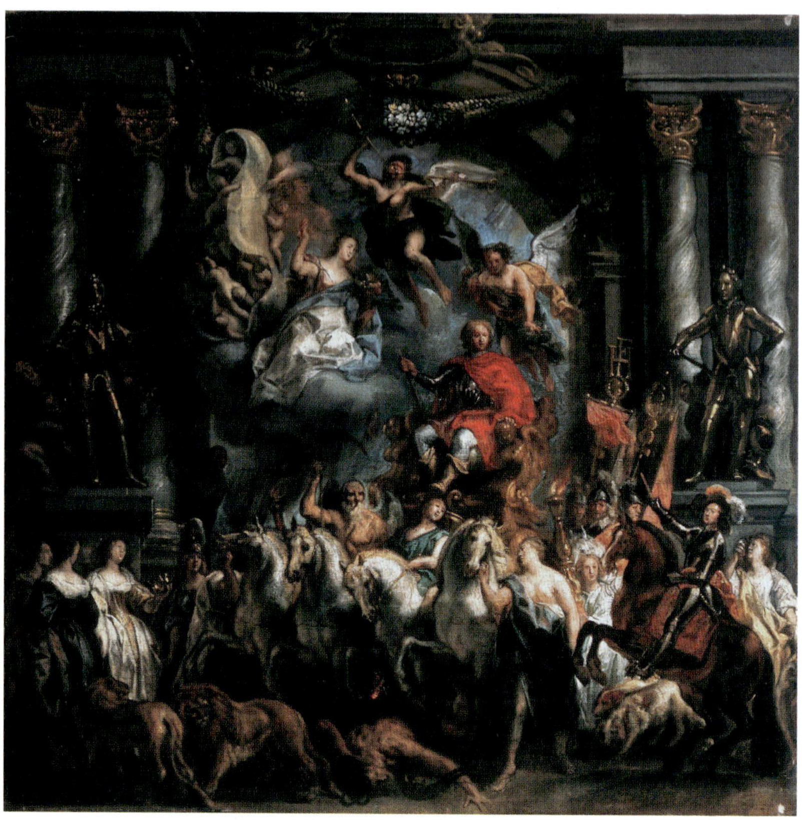

indicates in his letters that he will use a portrait of Frederik Hendrik by Honthorst for a better likeness.

Jordaens shows the late stadholder as the focal point of a complex allegorical triumph. Frederik Hendrik appears as the highest figure, riding like a Roman emperor in a chariot drawn by a quadriga of white horses and visible at full length while seated on a gilded throne. Like a conquering hero, he is about to pass under a massive triumphal arch that has flanking statues in armour of William the Silent and Maurits, his

44 Jacob Jordaens, *Triumph of Frederik Hendrik, Modello for Oranjezaal, Huis ten Bosch, The Hague*, 1651, oil on canvas.

predecessors as stadholder. He is backed by the hovering winged figure of Nike, or Victory, who places a laurel wreath of conquest on his head and holds another for his successor. That figure is his son and heir (although he died young in 1650), William II, who appears in armour directly below Frederik Hendrik on horseback, again rearing in levade to show his prowess as both an equestrian and military commander. Also hovering about Frederik Hendrik is the winged figure of Fame, blowing her trumpets, and Irene, goddess of peace, holding a palm branch and a horn of plenty. Putti in a golden light at the top of the canvas hover with attributes of the Seven Liberal Arts, indicating the flourishing of the arts under the reign of Frederik Hendrik. Meanwhile, various Olympian gods guide the chariot: Neptune with his trident sits below the stadholder, indicating his leadership of the powerful Dutch navy, while Mercury the god of commerce and intelligence together with Chronos with his hourglass bestride two of the white horses. Alongside the quadriga the goddess of wisdom Minerva appears in armour to lead the steeds on the far side, while Hygeia, goddess of health, appears on the near flank at the foreground. The army follows the chariot, which is led by two powerful lions and greeted in front by loyal subjects of both sexes and a range of ages, also waving palms of peace. Probably at the suggestion of van Campen Jordaens altered some of these details in the final picture and turned the entry to a more frontal passage through the great arch while adding even more figures.

Thus the Huis ten Bosch is informed by the legacy of Rubens, especially for mythic figures used as allegories in such late works as his designs for the 1635 Antwerp *Triumph of Cardinal-Infante Ferdinand*, the regent of the Southern Netherlands. Rembrandt had nothing to contribute to such conceptions, although he came closest in the *Concord of the State*. But the Dutch vocabulary remained far more grounded in naturalistic representation, even on commission from Orange patrons. For example, one Honthorst canvas, undated, depicts Artemisia (*c.* 1630–35), the ancient world's paragon of married female virtue, who erected for her deceased husband Mausolus (d. 352 BCE) the celebrated Mausoleum of Halicarnassus, one of the seven wonders of the ancient world. According to legend, recorded by Valerius Maximus, the widow, wearing the black veil of mourning, accepted the ashes of her cremated husband in a goblet. (During his own flirtation with the Orange court Rembrandt also painted an *Artemisia*, 1634, a half-length figure for an unknown patron.) While Honthorst perhaps painted his picture earlier, possibly even for Elizabeth of Bohemia as widow of the Winter King, it is already recorded as a chimneypiece in an early inventory of the Huis ten Bosch.

Amalia van Solms did commission an allegory about her own widowhood from Rembrandt's own former apprentice from around 1633 (the time of Rembrandt's own Passion series for the stadholder), Govert Flinck, who soon afterwards would succeed him as master of the Uylenburgh studio. Soon after this court painting, Flinck, 'the epitome of a cultured artist', would also become the principal painter commissioned to decorate the Amsterdam Town Hall, cut short only by his untimely death. The contrast between Rembrandt's religious work and the sentiments of this *Amalia van Solms Mourning for her Husband, Frederik Hendrik* (1654; illus. 45) could not be more stark. Amalia is portrayed as pious widow, sitting in mourning black before the elaborate, multi-figure, sculpted tomb ensemble of her late husband, adorned with the allegories of both Justice and Fortitude. She shares an open book on her lap, presumably the accounts of his historical achievements and triumphs as ruler. Her allegorical companion is a helmeted young woman wearing a laurel wreath of glory and carrying a palm branch of peace (in tribute to the recent 1648 Peace of Westphalia), Amalia gazes in front of her at a young woman who kneels, echoing the traditional posture of the angel of the Annunciation to the Virgin Mary, while holding a symbolic anchor, attribute of the virtue of Hope (as in Pieter Bruegel's allegory of that virtue). She also carries the sprig from an orange tree, symbolic of the recent birth of the young Orange heir and future stadholder as William III, born just after the sudden death of his father William II. Finally, at the left edge an angel rushes in while signalling that the storm clouds above are now parting in the upper left corner to admit beams of heavenly light, the promise of a brighter future under divine sanction for the new ruler-to-be. Finally, a phoenix resurrected from its own ashes appears in the central distance, to confirm that the House of Orange would rise again. (Rembrandt also produced an etching in 1658, *The Phoenix*, B. 110, possibly suggesting his own lingering Orangist sympathies, broached earlier – if more ambiguously – in the *Concord of the State*.)

Flinck's painting was intended for the decorations of the private apartment gallery at the Huis ten Bosch, framed with Corinthian pilasters on pedestals by Pieter Post. There it hung opposite an *Annunciation* by Willeboirts Bosschaert and a

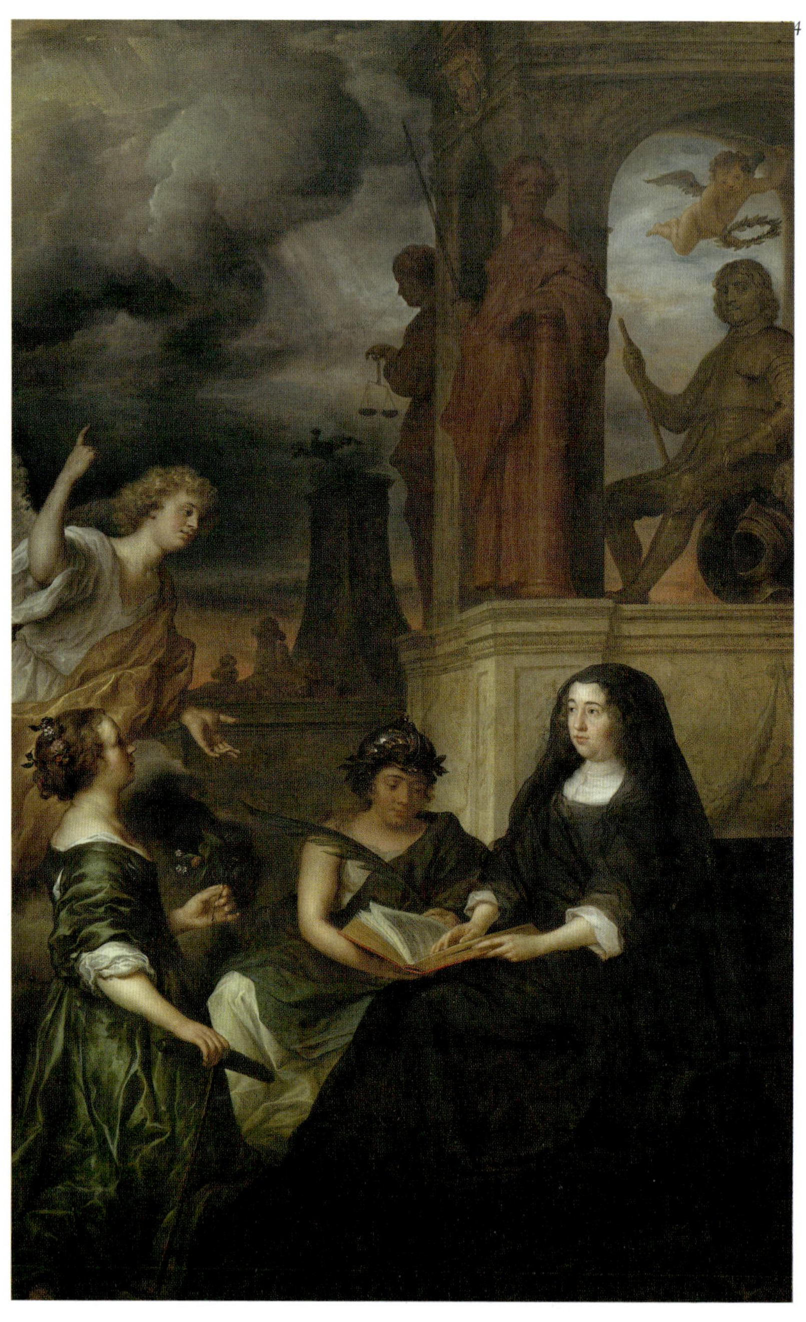

45 Govert Flinck, *Amalia van Solms Mourning for Her Husband, Frederick Hendrick*, 1654, oil on canvas.

second painting by him (with Daniel Seghers) of the *Madonna in a Flower Garland* (which included oranges). Paintings of the other six virtues decorated the doors, but Hope abides with Amalia van Solms and with the nation, now politically independent at last. Once again, this court picture draws on the heritage of Rubens, specifically his tribute to the widowed queen mother of France, Marie de' Medici (1622–5; Louvre), which combined portraits of the regent and widow with both mythic and allegorical figures. Like that cycle by Rubens, this painting by Flinck signals optimism in the face of events, for this was the 'stadholderless' period of Dutch history.

The careers of Flinck as well as Jacob van Campen culminated in Amsterdam with the construction after 1648 of the Town Hall there (see illus. 3), truly a 'palace for the people'. Van Campen, who left the project in 1654, was assisted by Pieter Post and by city architect Daniel Stalpaert. Together they produced one of Europe's grandest buildings, hailed by contemporaries as the 'eighth wonder of the world'. Stately corridors extend from the towering, double-storeyed central hall, the Burgerzaal ('Citizens' Hall'), to rows of large rooms arrayed around two symmetrical courtyards. The basement houses a prison and a Hall of Judgment for public pronouncements of death sentences. As at other seventeenth-century classicizing buildings, the Amsterdam Town Hall presents monumental pediments both on its projecting main facade on the Dam Square but also on its rear side. The entire structure is knitted together by colossal order Corinthian pilasters within projecting pavilions at the corners. Crowning the public face of the building is a tall cupola, which lightens the effect of its mass.

To decorate the interior required appropriately classical monumental sculpture. Luxurious works by Flemish masters were led by the Flemish workshop of Artus Quellinus from Antwerp, who had also worked in Rome. He adorned interior rooms, such as the Solomon relief amid virtues of Justice and Prudence in the Hall of Judgement; he also designed the pediments, whose allegories show (front) sea gods paying homage to Amsterdam and (rear) the Four Continents bringing both goods and homage to the figure of Amsterdam. His massive marble figure of Atlas bent under the globe with spread arms caps the frieze of the Burgerzaal, and a bronze version adorns the rear pediment.

We have already seen how the Amsterdam Town Hall paintings decorating chambers utilized Old Testament biblical subjects to make an inspiring link between the Dutch present and the Chosen People (for example, for the Alderman's Chamber, *Moses with the Tablets of the Law*, 1659, by Ferdinand Bol, another former Rembrandt pupil; see illus. 18). For another council-chamber setting Flinck produced a major painting with a similar theme, his *Solomon's Prayer for Wisdom* (1659), for which, like Jordaens, he also made an oil sketch. Backed by the high priest, the wisest of kings of Israel is shown praying to God while kneeling before a sacrificial altar and asking for guidance as a ruler (1 Kings 3:9). Flinck shows heaven responding directly to his prayer through the personification of Wisdom, hovering on clouds and surrounded by cherubs. A host of other angels, playing musical instruments, descends in light on clouds in the top centre. Characteristically, as with Bol's painting, the leading contemporary Dutch poets, Joost van den Vondel and Jan Vos, wrote poems celebrating this same biblical imagery.

Rembrandt's one contribution to the larger Town Hall decoration, his large canvas, *The Oath of Claudius Civilis* (1661, see illus. 19), was designed to fill the massive lunettes at the ends of galleries surrounding the central Burgerzaal. But it was rejected and replaced, for reasons that remain uncertain, and eventually it was cut down to be salvaged. The larger theme of the lunettes was the revolt of the ancient ancestors of the Dutch, the Batavians, who revolted against occupying Roman legions, as recounted in the *Histories* by Tacitus. While his earthy, indecorous presentation of the half-blind national hero might in itself have been enough reason to find Rembrandt's work unacceptable, Margaret Carroll suggests that Rembrandt's politics might also have played a large role. In this case, he would have upset local civic leaders for his insufficient support of the Amsterdam faction favouring the Orangists. Some resistance to his seeming debasement of Claudius Civilis may also have come from the artist's ongoing tensions with the De Graeff family, including burgomaster Cornelis, who devised the newer Batavian iconographic programme and shifted Amsterdam politics closer to the Orange sympathizers, who saw their own heroic war for independence foreshadowed by the Batavians. Flinck would have been the ideal painter for such a cycle at that moment. Vondel's verse caption about the *Oath*, anticipating a heroic presentation of ancient republican ritual, reads:

> Here you see in Civilis the greatness of Orange.
> He entered into a sworn alliance and turned against
>   Rome.
> So turned William in his armor against Spain.
> Freedom long suppressed now speaks out loud.

Graeff's brother Andries also supported Jan Lievens as well as Jacob Jordaens for concurrent commissions on the project to replace Flinck. Lievens did paint a large related subject, *Brinio Raised on a Shield* (also 1661), a scene of heroic leadership acclamation from the Batavian Revolt, but showing a second commander who was selected by his people instead of by noble heredity. Both that scene and Rembrandt's *Oath* were originally sketched for realization by Flinck before his death in February 1660.

But like the *Concord of the State*, Rembrandt's *Oath* seems to have straddled both viewpoints regarding the Dutch Revolt in its ancestry. While he portrayed the solemnity of the sword-oath and showed the central figure of Civilis as crowned, even royal, he still gave his face a late-style focus that is both unheroic and brutal, at once rough and simple in both brushwork and visage. Consequently, Rembrandt seems to have simultaneously violated everyone's sense of the decorum of this crucial subject. Little wonder that Rembrandt's representation of this rude, pagan *Oath* inevitably failed to find favour with either faction.

By 1662 the political tide had fully turned, and old antipathies between city and court were restored, so that Rembrandt's *Civilis* could then be viewed from a civic perspective as too pro-Orange, even royalist. Thus the replacement canvas by Jürgen Ovens (1662), a pupil of Flinck, perhaps painted over outlines of Flinck's original design, restored the multi-figured array across the table, displacing Civilis in Roman armour and profile pose to the far right, gesturing to heaven under a crescent moon, but clearly less regal and no longer dominating the composition. The Batavian leader now is reduced to *primus inter pares*.

Only a few years later, Rembrandt returned twice to a single-figure theme from history: the *Suicide of Lucretia* (1664; 1666; see illus. 46). The two paintings, whose patrons are unknown, show a before-and-after sequence, where each woman holds the knife of her undoing at different moments of the narrative. The earlier canvas (Washington) shows the agonized self-awareness of the heroine before she plunges the knife into her body, whereas the calmer, more ruminative later work (Minneapolis) follows her action to its denouement, marked by the spreading bloodstain on her tunic. These late works fully display the virtuoso variety of applying thick pigment with a palette knife, especially in the sleeves, contrasted with the fine, layered brushwork of the faces and hands. Dramatic lighting and chiaroscuro heighten the suggestion of inner mental life. This intense focus on the gestures and facial expressions of a figure seen at half-length isolation against a dark background recalls paintings by Caravaggio or his Utrecht followers, such as Honthorst and ter Bruggen.

The story derives from ancient Roman history. As recounted by Livy (I, 57–60), Lucretia, celebrated for her virtue and fidelity, inspired the lust of visiting Sextus Tarquinius, son of the tyrannical ruler of Rome in the late sixth century BCE. He stole into her chamber and threatened to kill her if she did not yield to him, an offence that would have been even more heinous had he fulfilled his threat to kill his own slave and place the body beside her in double dishonour. Although Lucretia did yield to this rape from Tarquin, she assembled her father and husband the next day and told her story, saying that she preferred death to dishonour before taking her own life with a knife. That is the moment that Rembrandt addresses, following Italian precedents in prints, such as an engraving by Marcantonio Raimondi after Raphael (*c.* 1511–12). But other artists (Titian; Tintoretto) favoured the rape scene, or else artists such as Lucas Cranach in Luther's Germany used the suicide as an occasion to feature the voluptuous beauty of Lucretia as a snare to tempt the viewer as much as Tarquin. The heroine also appears in triads of Worthy Women, both in prints and paintings, along with other ancient Roman paragons of virtue, Virginia and Veturia (or Cloelia).

The denouement of Livy's story also held political resonance, however, because Lucretia's suicide sparked her family's revenge against the Tarquin dynasty, whose overthrow led to the establishment of the Roman Republic. This overthrow of tyranny had the effect of political change and newfound freedom. Dutch artists understood that significance as well; during the intense early phase of the Dutch Revolt, printmaker Hendrick Goltzius made a Lucretia cycle of four engravings of the story (*c.* 1578–80), which ends with the suicide scene and the subsequent military gathering, visible in the distance. A poem by Jan Vos about a painting of Lucretia by Flinck underscores the same message: 'In the red ink she writes a definition of freedom.'

By choosing such a momentous spur to liberation and freedom, Rembrandt might have been simply repeating the celebration of independence that Goltzius meant with his earlier print cycle. But his message remains ambiguous to the end: whether freedom in this case could reinforce the free trade and civic independence of the larger cities, led by Amsterdam, or else be addressed to the patriotic spirit that

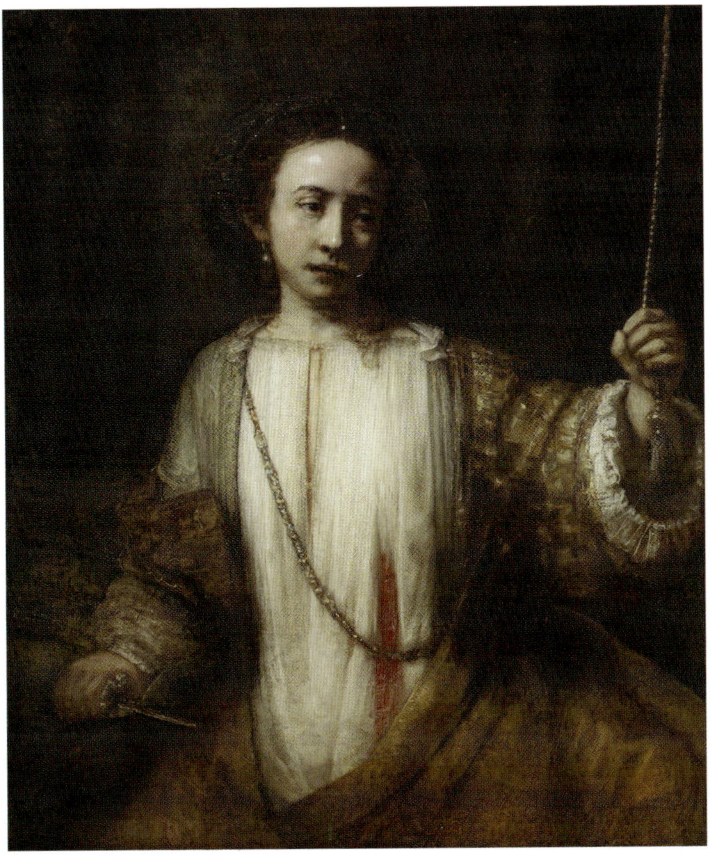

motivated the Orange party. Once more, as with both the *Concord of the Land* or even the *Oath of Claudius Civilis*, we can see Rembrandt engaged with contemporary issues of politics and freedom, but to specify his party affiliation, despite repeated claims about his Orange sympathies, remains ambiguous throughout.

At the same time many interpreters have read Rembrandt's choice of the Lucretia theme in biographical terms. His

46 Rembrandt, *Suicide of Lucretia*, 1666, oil on canvas.

common-law wife, Hendrickje Stoffels, died of plague in 1663, and her steadfast support, conjugal (despite her troubles in 1654 with the Calvinist elders over living in sin) as well as financial, in her final decade with the artist surely played a part in his empathy for his depictions of this anguished ancient pillar of virtue. His Lucretias remain chastely dressed, even in death, conscious agents of their own tragic destiny. In half a decade, Rembrandt himself would die as well, but not before he had painted several of his most moving self-portraits, after three decades of self-expression.

FOUR

Rembrandt's World

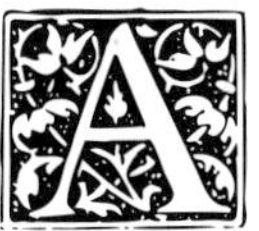S NOTED IN THE PREVIOUS CHAPTER, during the second quarter of the seventeenth century (1630–54) the Netherlands briefly extracted the segment of northeast Brazil as a colony from its habitual possessor Portugal, and in 1636 stadholder Frederik Hendrik's cousin, count Johan Maurits of Nassau-Siegen (owner of the Mauritshuis), was appointed its governor. He remained at his post until 1644, administering the region for the Dutch West India Company (founded in 1621) and its chief export commodity, one of the new food crazes of Europe: sugar. To man those sugar plantations, where local Indian labour did not suffice, the Dutch began to import slaves from Africa, soon shipped regularly from former Portuguese slave forts along the Gold Coast (chiefly in modern Ghana). The Dutch slave trade would persist well into the nineteenth century.

Along with his building of a new capital, Mauritsstad, at the Brazilian site, Johan Maurits also had particular interests in surveying and studying the new colony, its sites as well as its fauna and flora. To that end, he sponsored artists and scientists — and some artist-scientists — to accompany his voyage. They were led by painter Albert Eckhout (c. 1607–c. 1666), who made life-sized, paired, individual studies, male plus female, of the various Amerindian tribes and a pair of Africans, as well as numerous canvases and study sheets of exotic animals and indigenous foodstuffs. Naturalist and painter Georg Marcgraf and physician Willem Piso used those studies in publishing a scientific study, *Historia naturalis Brasiliae* (Amsterdam, 1648). Its frontispiece, based on Eckhout's painted studies, features a pair of flanking local Indians, standing naked before a lush tropical landscape, full of animals: anteater, sloth, tortoise, monkeys and parrots. Additionally a 1647 history of Dutch Brazil, *Rerum per octennium in Brasília*, was produced by Caspar Barlaeus in Amsterdam. Maps of the region by Marcgraf, which reinforced Dutch colonial claims, were sent back to Amsterdam, where they formed part of the leading map compendium, culminating in the great *Atlas maior* of Joan Blaeu (Amsterdam, 1665).

One of Johan Maurits's most influential painters made nothing but landscape views of Brazil, both during his time there and long after he returned to Holland and settled in Haarlem. Frans Post (1612–1680), the younger brother of prominent architect Pieter Post, remained with the governor, returning with him as well in 1644. He provided illustrations for Barlaeus's 1647 history of the colony. A Post sketchbook survives along with a mere seven on-site Brazil paintings, four of them in the Louvre as a result of an aristocratic gift from Maurits to Louis XIV of France in 1678 (most of his Eckhout paintings were presented already in 1656 to his cousin, Frederik III of Denmark). For the most part those first landscapes are careful topographic records, composed with characteristic Dutch low horizons, but organized as views across rivers and open waterways, partly for tactical usefulness in defence as

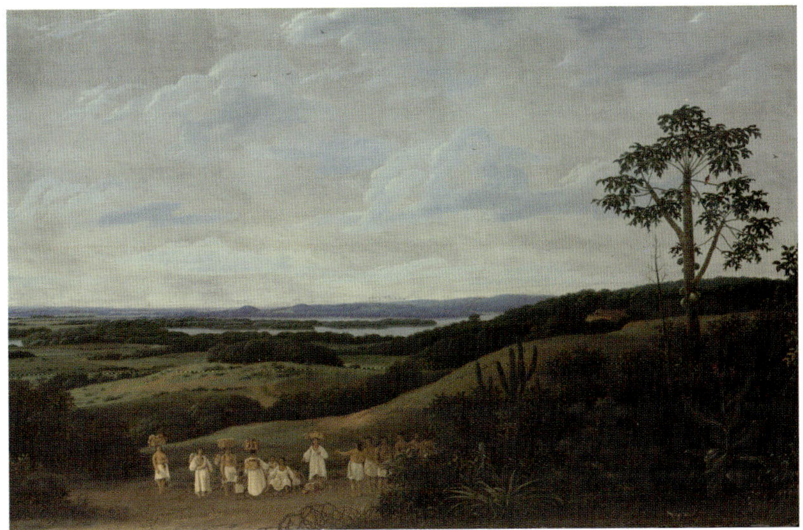

well as picturesque qualities, such as local animals and plants
inhabiting the foreground jungle growth (for example, *São
Francisco River with Fort Maurits*, 1638).

Post, however, continued to produce Brazil-inspired landscapes according to his own well-established pictorial formulas
until his last dated work of 1669, and several of his views of
plantations and landscapes were merged onto the open spaces
of Blaeu's Brazil maps as early as 1646. Much more typical of
the images made back home is Post's *Brazilian Landscape* (1650;
illus. 47). It uses the convention for showing depth and atmosphere by means of layers: placing the widest range of colours
in the foreground, greens with yellows, with a darker green
foreground of thick vegetation in the corner, where he also
places exotic animals (here an iguana; elsewhere a giant anteater, sloth or armadillo) as well as plants: cacti, coconuts or,
here, a ripening pineapple on its stalk. The narrow atmospheric

47 Frans Post, *Brazilian Landscape*, 1650, oil on wood.

distance, at the horizon beyond the open water and the marshland known as *varzea*, bathes in a uniform haze of monochromatic blue. Many of Post's scenes of plantations feature black African slaves, usually in unthreatening moments of leisure, such as a dance, but never with the backbreaking and life-shortening work that filled their days. In this New York canvas, he shows instead the peaceful local 'mission Indian' population, the Tupinamba. The women are decorously dressed in long provided garments (like those in Eckhout's life-sized Tupinamba couple, Copenhagen, where the gendered roles are the same) but several are topless; the men in white shorts are carrying their own arms, bow and arrows. All are immersed in the verdant, idyllic landscape panorama, serving as bearers for the plantation owner – and also seen from a privileged elevated viewpoint by the viewer. By implication these Tupis are assimilating into European behaviour and colonial service.

Frans Post's steady output of landscape paintings, based on experience of Brazil, however formulaic in execution, brought the exotic world of South America home to the Dutch, whose WIC and VOC were busy opening and securing foreign colonies across the southern hemisphere, including the lucrative Spice Islands in Southeast Asia. Beginning with the *Itinerario*, an illustrated volume with accounts about India, published in Amsterdam in 1596 by Jan Huygen van Linschoten, a century of travel books emerged to inform and entertain Dutch readers (and wider European audiences as well, like the maps of the world that emerged from Blaeu and Dutch presses). Linschoten had lived with the Portuguese archbishop in their colony in Goa on the coast of India, and his book not only aroused curiosity but revealed map secrets that served the VOC voyages shortly afterwards. His descriptions and etched illustrations (by the Doetecum brothers) of Asia's productive plants offered both scientific knowledge and practical uses for Dutch audiences.

From such sources, including the island sources for expensive nutmeg and mace imports, naturalists received numerous specimens of both animals and plants, which they increasingly assembled into collections known as 'cabinets of curiosity' (*Wunderkammer*). While these collections originally were the prerogatives of noblemen or rich merchants, in the Netherlands they became associated with scholars, such as Bernardus Paludanus, a botanist and physician in the port city of Enkhuizen, who worked closely with Linschoten on the botanical information in his *Itinerario* and whose own renowned collection was sold to a German nobleman, Friedrich, Duke of Württemberg-Teck. Such items also appear on display in one of the paintings of the Oranjezaal at the Huis ten Bosch, Jacob van Campen's *Triumphal Arch with Goods from the East and West*: exotic birds, Brazilian artefacts and even Chinese porcelains, which appear frequently in Dutch still-lifes. The English diarist John Evelyn records in 1641 how he purchased maps in the shops of atlas publishers Hondius and Blaeu as well as 'some shells and Indian curiosities'.

That aura of the gentleman-collector surely influenced Rembrandt's outlook on the influx of objects and information into Amsterdam from the far reaches of the globe. The artist's 1656 bankruptcy inventory makes clear that Rembrandt too was an avid collector, not only of artwork but of diverse exotic objects, including weapons, land and sea animals, and horns, along with an art study collection of paintings, prints, drawings and even antique sculpture (cf. the bust in his 1653 *Aristotle Contemplating the Bust of Homer*, New York; or the little etching, *c.* 1641, *Man Drawing from a Cast*, B. 130). Rembrandt's own drawn oeuvre certainly offers examples of specific items that he studied from his personal collection.

In 1650 Rembrandt meticulously etched a South Pacific shell, a *Conus marmoreus* (illus. 48), named for the marble-like effect of its brown-and-white pattern. It likely formed part of his art cabinet, which included 'a large quantity of horns, marine plants'. Similar rare shells appear in still-life paintings with costly flowers by specialists, especially Balthasar van der Ast (whose Rotterdam shell painting includes another *conus marmoreus* among numerous other specimens) and his

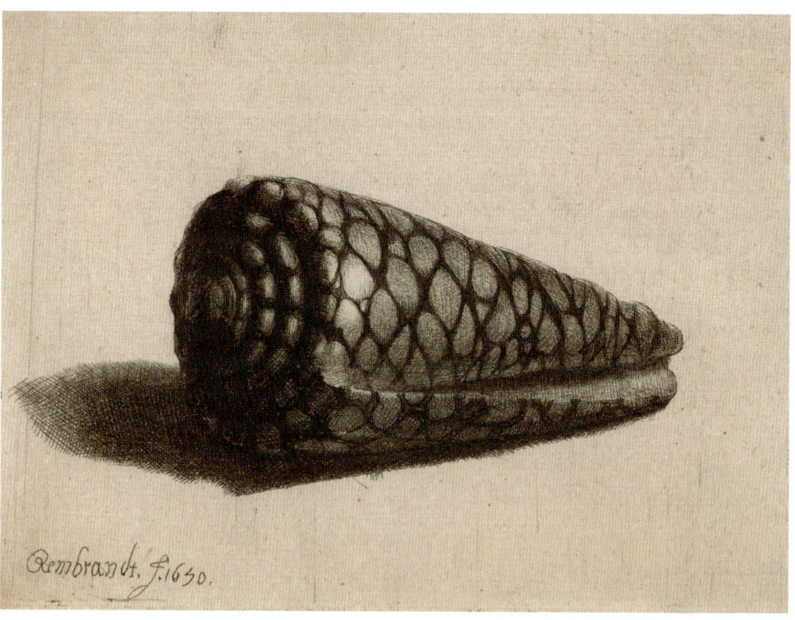

48 Rembrandt, *The Shell (Conus marmoreus)*, 1650, etching.

brother-in-law Ambrosius Bosschaert. One proud collector from the period of Paludanus, Jan Govertsen, even commissioned a portrait with his prize objects by Hendrick Goltzius (1603). Shells, in fact, show the artifice and beauty in nature itself, making them perfect additions to a *Wunderkammer* collection. But like the coveted tulip bulbs that sparked a buying craze that ended in a bubble crash in 1637, shells also drew inflated prices due to rarity and keen demand by collectors. In response, one illustrated emblem book, *Sinne-Poppen* by Roemer Visscher (first edition 1614), satirizes this phenomenon as folly, showing a cluster of exotic shells with the Dutch caption 'It's astonishing what use a fool can make with his money,' and also declaring that their 'only beauty is their rarity'. Thus shells in art conveyed their own coveted status but also the potential for the very folly involved in the high cost of collecting them.

Shells also could easily be understood as *vanitas* symbols, images that underscore the inevitable mortality of all living things. They would thus figure like the skull or bones within those warning still-lifes, also laden with hourglasses, watches or soap bubbles. In addition, alongside either flowers or fruit in other still-lifes, shells further reinforce their fragile, perishable beauty.

Rembrandt's *Shell* is a virtuoso graphic work which raises many of these possible layers of interpretation. An etching whose artistry captures the artistry of nature, it sets off the prized object as the sole focus. It puts the shell and its cast shadow into a shallow space, delineated with rich, velvety blacks and subtly differentiated patches that model the white portions of the shell itself. Documents reveal that Rembrandt also paid high prices for such objects, notably a conch shell. Making an etching of a shell had a recent precedent (though never published): Wenceslaus Hollar made another virtuoso set of shell etchings, without settings or shadows, in 1646 for his patron, the major collector (especially of drawings by Leonardo and Holbein, also etched then by Hollar) and exiled Marshal of England, Thomas Howard, Earl of Arundel. But Rembrandt's *Shell* remains unique in his printed oeuvre, and it is not nearly as useful as a scientific image as comparable paintings or even Hollar's prints (indeed, scholars have observed that the spiral of the shell's pattern is represented backwards, anticlockwise, in the etching).

Rembrandt's fascination for the wider natural world endured, however. His 1656 collection inventory lists a book 'filled with drawings by Rembrandt of animals done from life'. A rare signed and dated elephant drawing of 1637 in black chalk, reinforced with charcoal shadows, uses swift sure strokes to suggest the rough skin surface and the turn of the agile trunk; three other chalk drawings focus on details of profile and front legs, clearly indicating that the artist made these studies from a living animal that he had occasion to encounter. Rembrandt would soon afterwards incorporate such an elephant as an isolated background feature in his Eden setting for a 1638 etching of the *Fall of Mankind* (B. 28). Around the same time Rembrandt also used the chalk medium with charcoal in two studies of lionesses, reinforced with grey wash, possibly from the menagerie of Frederik Hendrik in The Hague. This creature, in turn, was adapted for the political allegory of the shorn lion as Leo Belgicus in Rembrandt's oil sketch, no. 106 in the 1656 inventory, *The*

Concord of the State (c. 1640; see illus. 42). Camels appear in the *Hundred-guilder Print* (c. 1648/9; see illus. 30) and *John the Baptist Preaching* (c. 1634; Berlin; see illus. 22).

Perhaps the most exotic animals ever recorded by Rembrandt are *Birds of Paradise*, two studies in pen with wash on a single sheet (c. 1640). In this case, we know that this very rare specimen from Papua New Guinea actually belonged to Rembrandt himself, a stuffed specimen recorded in a drawer ('a paradise bird and six fans') during the 1656 inventory. Like many early naturalists, including Conrad Gessner and Dutchman Carolus Clusius, Rembrandt shows these long-feathered birds without legs, because that was how they were shipped when mounted; consequently, early descriptions characterized birds of paradise as legless in life, so obliged to fly constantly. Such a considerable treasure from the East Indies, closely linked to the Dutch spice trade, would be a prize of Rembrandt's *Wunderkammer.*

Costumes, especially 'Oriental' or 'biblical' costumes, always fascinated Rembrandt. We observed in his *St John the Baptist Preaching* (see illus. 22) how many nationalities appear within the outdoor congregation in their native garb: turbans, headdresses and kaftans, plus Japanese armour, a popular collector's item. Additionally, the exotic curving blade that Rembrandt shows being used for *The Blinding of Samson* (1636; see illus. 40) is in fact a kris from Java. Among the varied items listed in 1656 was a book 'filled with curious drawings in miniature as well as woodcuts and engravings on copper of various costumes'. Thus Rembrandt drew inspiration for his costumes wherever he could find it, sometimes from collected objects but chiefly from artworks.

But one cluster of drawings by Rembrandt himself copies original album miniatures from the Mughal court of Agra, many of them still together now in the British Museum (*c.* 1655; illus. 49). Here the unusual profile stiffness and courtly ceremony of the figures complement their varied, foreign costumes, which Rembrandt simplifies with fine line work and light washes. In a number of cases, individual figures are recognizable; the features of Emperor Jahangir ('World-seizer'; *r.* 1605–27) in particular remains portrait-like, with distinctive jowls and drooping moustache. In this drawing, despite his kneeling posture on a divan, the emperor is larger physically, fully armed with sword and dagger, and more richly attired with an elaborate feathered turban that makes him taller still. He is clearly the superior figure, receiving homage and a written report from his subordinate officer. Several equestrian portraits from the Mughal album were also copied by the artist.

While Rembrandt seldom used any of his Mughal miniature copies for his public artwork, in one case, from his drawing *Four Orientals beneath a Tree*, he did adapt the costumed figure types for an etching: *Abraham and the Three Angels* (1656; B. 29). The original Mughal image behind his drawing has survived in the imperial collections of Vienna; it reveals some subtle changes by the artist but basic fidelity to his model. The 1656 dated etching, completed in the same year as the bankruptcy inventory, confirms that Rembrandt already had access to, or even possession of, this group of Mughal miniatures before then.

By far the largest portion of Rembrandt's personal collection, however, was art, chiefly in the form of prints and

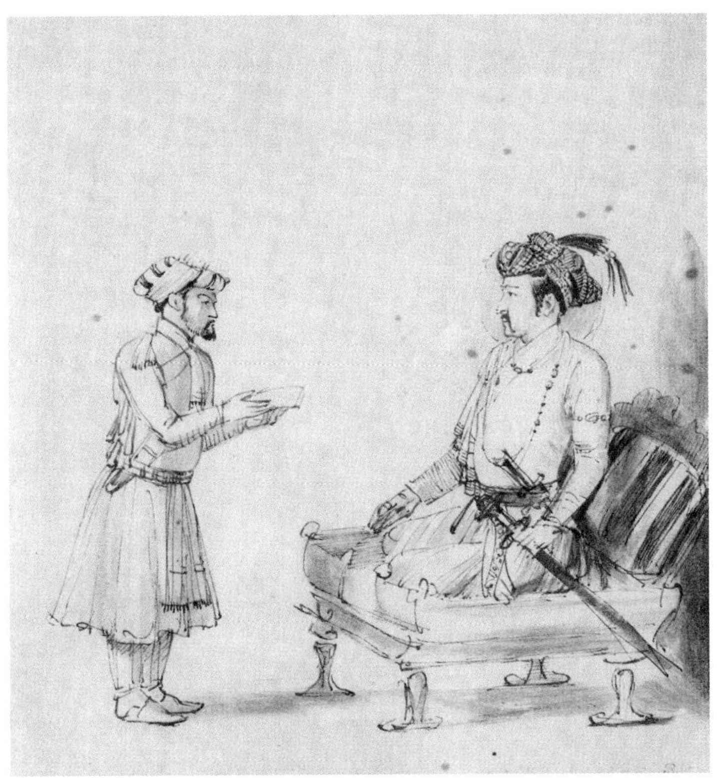

drawings by his revered models. He did keep a number of his own works in hand. Some, such as the *Concord of the State*, comprised unsold ventures, grisailles or other studies: landscapes, animals, studio models and heads, *tronies* (including two heads of Christ, nos. 115 and 118; see illus. 29). Works by other artists possibly made up stock available for resale; Rembrandt also invested in artwork as a sometime dealer. Two Italian paintings in the inventory (nos. 34, 109) are listed as jointly owned with known dealer Pieter de la Tombe. Many other Italian works are explicitly noted as copies. The bulk of his

49 Rembrandt, *Emperor Jahangir Receiving an Officer*, ink drawing with wash, *c.* 1655.

original paintings by Dutch or Flemish painters are all by the older generation, all deceased, and they may also have been acquired as sales inventory: genre scenes by Adriaen Brouwer, seascapes by Jan Porcellis and landscapes by Hercules Seghers, as well as varied images by his own former associate Jan Lievens.

Among the works of graphic art, Rembrandt's inventory scarcely mentions his prints, but 24 albums and two packets of his drawings are listed. Most of them are organized, like contemporary collections of prints, by subjects: figure studies, including nudes; animals; copies of sculptures and 'antique drawings'; landscapes. Most prized were prints by old masters, both German and Netherlandish (especially Lucas van Leyden but also Pieter Bruegel, Maarten van Heemskerck and the Hendrick Goltzius circle in Haarlem) and, especially 'precious', works by Italians in album 'books' (Mantegna, Raphael, Michelangelo and Titian as well as Antonio Tempesta). Some works on paper held value for their thematic content, such as scenic Tyrolean landscapes by Roelandt Savery, Turkish scenes by Melchior Lorck and erotic prints by Italians (Raphael, Rosso, Annibale Carracci and Giulio Bonasone).

One surviving pen sketch by Rembrandt reveals his ongoing keen interest in old master Italian paintings. It records a major art auction in Amsterdam on 9 April 1639 of the collection of Lucas van Uffelen, who had lived in Venice. There Rembrandt saw Raphael's *Baldassare Castiglione* portrait (*c.* 1515), which quickly influenced Rembrandt's own 1639 etched *Self-portrait* (see illus. 54) and then his closely related 1640 painted *Self-portrait* (London, National Gallery). Rembrandt annotated the drawing, which he modified with a prominent arm resting on the balustrade of another painting, Titian's early *Man with a Blue Sleeve* (c. 1511–12). He also recorded the hefty sale price, an astonishing 3,500 guilders (Rembrandt received 1,600 guilders for his *Nightwatch* group portrait), as it was sold to diamond merchant Alphonso Lopez, who already owned the Titian. With Amsterdam's flourishing art market, Rembrandt's reply to Constantijn Huygens seems more justified: he did not need to go to Italy, as Huygens urged, because in effect the best of Italy was then coming up to Holland.

Rembrandt certainly wanted to be known by his first name, like the Italians, whether Raphael or Michelangelo, so he started after 1633, early in his Amsterdam career, to sign that way instead of the RHL initials of his Leiden period. The saga of the critical fortunes of his career has often been told, but the basic outline remains that Rembrandt came in for criticism by some authors in his later phases for his lack of finish and his lack of ideals, which failed to impress the classicizing trends in Dutch art, especially after mid-century, codified in the treatise by painter Gerard de Lairesse *Groot Schilderboeck* (Large Book of Painting). But as Eric Jan Sluijter has reasserted, Rembrandt seriously strove to compete with his great predecessors like Raphael, Titian and, of course, Rubens, even though his earthy nudes mark his personal, distinctive departure from their ideal models.

What Rembrandt thought privately of his critics emerges from a relatively early vicious *Satire on Criticism* (1644; illus. 50), where he penned another rare inscription. Seated on an empty barrel, suggesting a tavern setting, and pontificating with a pipe – itself an image of transient smoke as well as idleness – an ass-eared critic gestures towards a framed

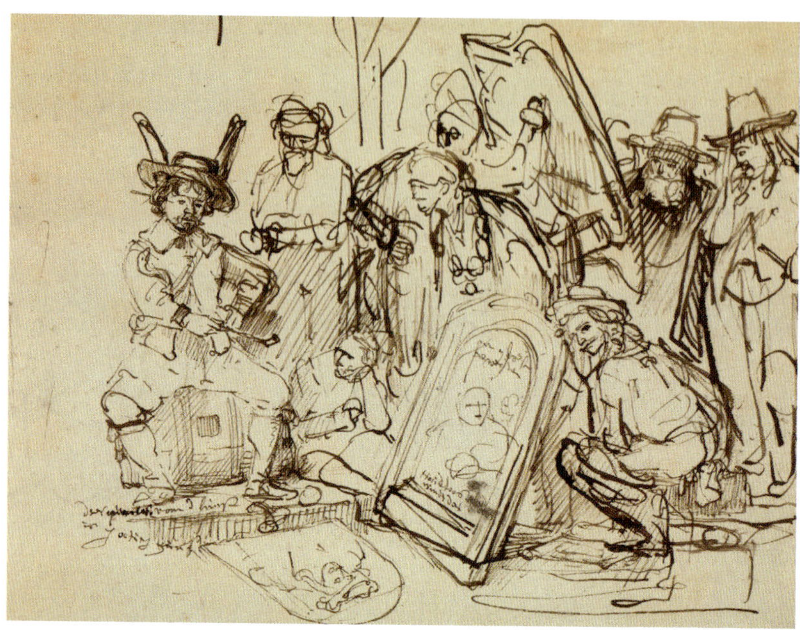

half-length portrait painting that rests on the floor. A second half-length portrait with a rounded top rests at his feet. This critic does not even wear the pince-nez glasses that sit at his feet, so his short-sightedness is doubly reinforced. Neverthe-less, a crowd gathers to listen attentively to his words; one of them, holding the framed image under consideration, wears a chain with large discs, as if he were a court artist with a princely award or at least a leading guild official. At the upper right two well-dressed men in contemporary hats peer at a shield-like object, perhaps another painting, held up behind the framed picture, for them to consider buying. Ernst van de Wetering associates this group of onlookers with the con-noisseurs or *liefhebbers* (literally amateurs, or lovers, of art), who began to associate closely with artists in both Holland

50 Rembrandt, *Satire on Criticism*, 1644, ink drawing.

and Flanders during this century. Their naivety and gullibility before would-be critics or theorists of art has become an object of scorn for the true artist in the corner. But one major figure dissents, squatting and shitting in the lower right corner behind the painting in question. He looks out at the viewer as if seeking confirmation from a fellow-traveller as he wipes his behind with a sheet of paper, like the support for this very drawing or possibly instead a page torn from the published theories of such would-be critics.

The slightly archaic dress of the assed-eared pontificator and the looping first '4' in the date of 1644 might also link this image to the foundational text of art theory and art history in the Netherlands, the *Schilderboek*, or Book of Painting, by painter-theorist Karel van Mander, published in 1604 in Haarlem. At the time of this drawing the most prominent art theory was Franciscus Junius's *The Painting of the Ancients in Three Books*, first published in Amsterdam in 1637, then in English and Dutch translations in 1641, so Rembrandt might have been targeting that prescriptive work. And he does so precisely with his own self-conscious breach of pictorial decorum that his critics attacked most severely.

A similarly private, even intimate, drawing with quite the opposite intent was produced by Rembrandt only a few years later. In 1652 for the personal gift album, or *album amicorum*, of his patrician patron Jan Six (see the etched portrait, illus. 13; also a painted half-length, 1654), he offered his own visual tribute amidst the other dedicated poems, epigrams, emblems and autographs, dated and signed to his friend, his only drawing with a dedication, 'Rembrandt to Joanus Six.1652' (illus. 51). This work represents a classical subject appropriate to the learned Six: blind Homer reciting outdoors to a responsive crowd of listeners. Moreover, this composition, extending downward to a lower level, responds to a sanctioned old master model: Raphael's *Parnassus*, engraved by Marcantonio Raimondi after the design for the 1511 fresco mural in the papal library in Rome, the Stanza della Segnatura. In fact, Raphael's image centres on the reclining god Apollo, master of the arts and leader of the muses, but it also features at its highest point the laureate figure of Homer, whose split-level listeners and flanking trees were retained but reversed by Rembrandt in his drawing.

In effect, whether because of the character of his patron or within the broadening cultural emphasis in Holland on classical forms and themes, Rembrandt turned towards both elements. Yet in comparison to the 1644 *Satire on Criticism*, *Homer Reciting* shows a broader, simplified outline style with earthier, more ungraceful figures, further emphasized by Rembrandt's choice of a stiff reed pen rather than the flexible quill that he used for earlier drawings. Like his late paintings, Rembrandt now reduces his imagery down to essentials, almost devoid of earlier gestures, to emphasize not action but thought, and to represent figures who listen carefully or speak softly. Even against the grain of prevailing taste for refinement and elaboration, he opts for sketchy suggestions of the unfinished, despite adding a frame for the drawing. This alternate form of virtuosity leaves some reading of the *non-finito* to the viewer. But such an unfinished or late style was already praised by Pliny's canonical discussion of ancient art in his *Natural History*, and even Franciscus Junius acknowledges the value of perceiving the inner thoughts and the

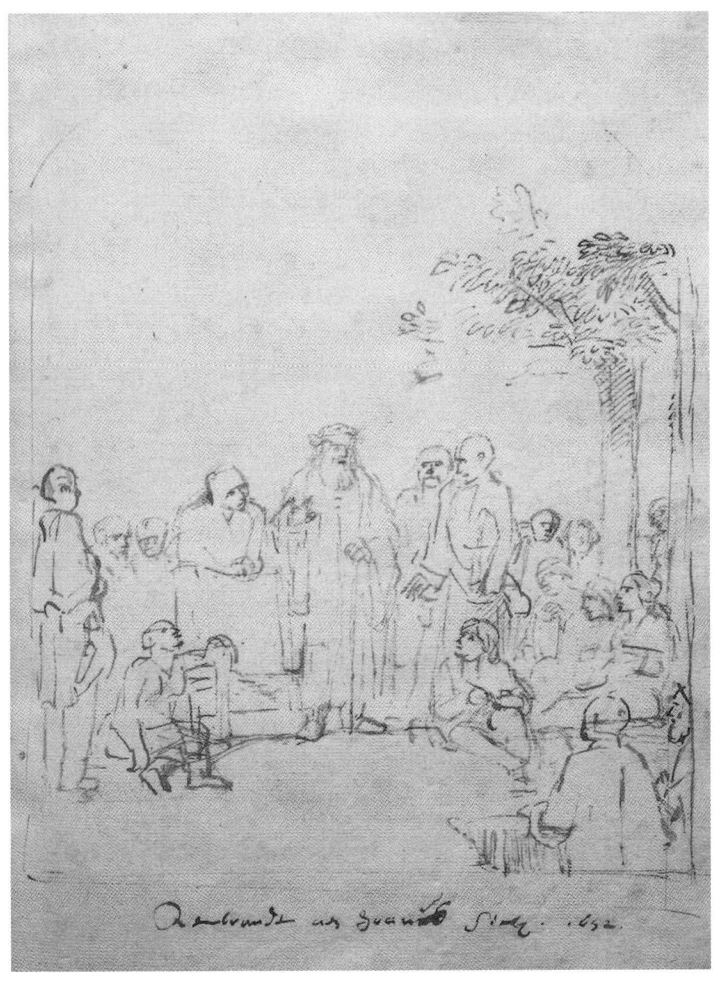

distinctive personal hand of an artist through such primary
designs. Thus Rembrandt devoted his work to Six with a
sophisticated, self-conscious early version of his emerging
late 'plain' style, while still paying homage to Raphael and to
classical subject-matter. Looking back, we can agree with

51 Rembrandt, *Homer Reciting Verses*, 1652, ink drawing.

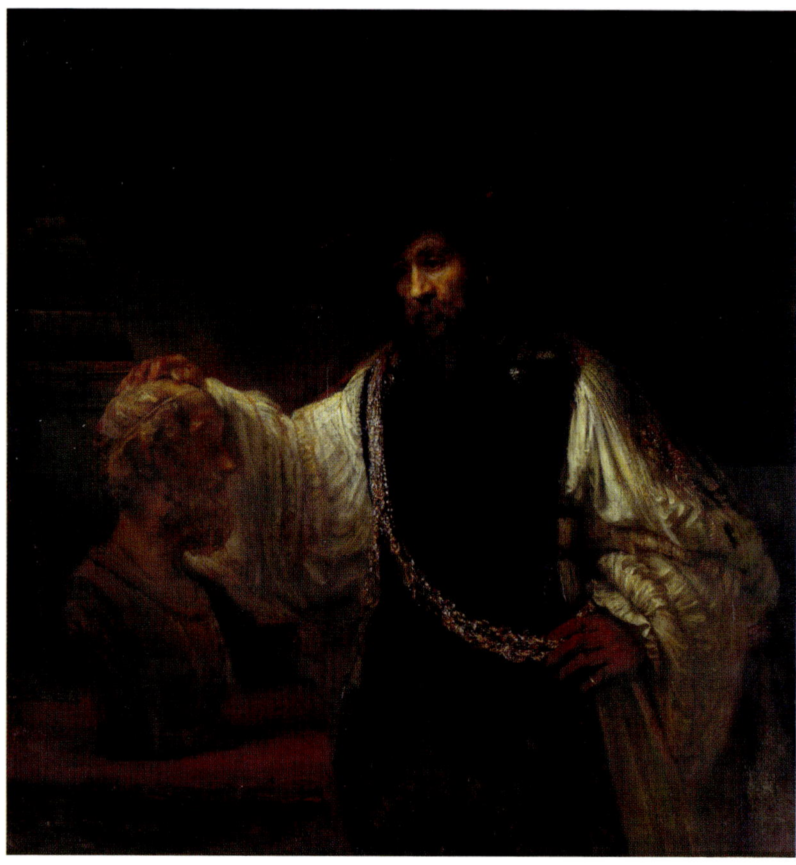

observers who have seen even in Rembrandt's copies after Mughal album miniatures the same kind of admiration for simplification and stillness.

The very next year another classical subject, *Aristotle Contemplating the Bust of Homer* (1653; illus. 52), employs Rembrandt's *rouw*, or rough, style in painting. It, too, had an intended patron, who only loosely determined the subject: Don Antonio Ruffo, a Sicilian nobleman from Messina, who mostly patronized

52 Rembrandt, *Aristotle Contemplating the Bust of Homer*, 1653, oil on canvas.

contemporary Italian painters like Guercino. The specifics of this topic were lost on its owner, who recorded its subject in his 1654 inventory only as 'a philosopher . . . Aristotle or Albertus Magnus'. Thus on some level, the fame of the artist determined the commission as much as the subject requested from him, though Rembrandt would have been known in Italy chiefly from his etchings, which Don Ruffo also collected. Later both Guercino and Rembrandt – with an *Alexander the Great* (lost; possibly associated with a 1655 canvas in Glasgow) and a *Homer Reciting* (1663, a damaged fragment) – were commissioned to provide complementary images for Don Ruffo.

Rembrandt shows off his learning by connecting the ancient author of the *Poetics* with the original epic poet, whose founding verses about tragic heroes contributed so much to later Greek literature, especially ancient Athenian tragic dramas, which form the core of the surviving *Poetics* treatise. Moreover, the depicted bust purporting to be the blind poet with a diadem is based on an actual surviving ancient Greek marble (now in Boston), part of the collection of ancient busts and casts from which both Rembrandt and his pupils studied; Rembrandt also reused that sculpted model later or his 1661 *Homer Reciting* for the same Don Ruffo.

But this *Aristotle*, quiet and thoughtful in the glowing golden chiaroscuro lighting of his study, held particular significance for the painter himself. Aristotle, we recall, was not just a renowned philosopher; he was also the tutor of Alexander the Great (perhaps the prompt for the additional commission from Don Ruffo of that historic figure). Indeed, close inspection of the almost relief-like chain around the neck of the philosopher reveals the profile of the ruler we can take to be his master, namely Alexander, since gold chains were a reward for princely service and were proudly worn in self-portraits by court artists such as Anthony van Dyck. Rembrandt even appended imaginary gold chains to his neck in a few early self-portraits, when he still avidly sought recognition and court artist status for his work. Rembrandt surely knew what worldly ambition could mean to a man, and in this painting he shows the philosopher psychologically torn – between his philosophical calling of a contemplative life versus the active commitment of a courtier, whose lavish costume, including the gold chain, marks his success and status. Thus the quiet, shadowed philosopher forms a middle term between the pure creativity of the poet (ironically, blind relative to the career of an artist) and the ruling warrior, and his dilemma emerges literally from his hands, at once touching the ancient bust and the modern chain of office. For an artist like Rembrandt, the path of Aristotle in 1653 represents the road not taken, the abandonment of earlier ambitions for court office and status in favour of the creative path, now becoming increasingly personalized and distinctive in contrast to the artistic leadership he had shown in earlier decades in Leiden and Amsterdam.

A recent suggestion that the 'Aristotle' figure might instead be Apelles, the exclusive painter of Alexander the Great known from the accounts of Pliny, has merit and would hold even more personal poignancy for Rembrandt as an artist; such a court chain would be equally appropriate for Apelles as for Aristotle. However, nothing connects Apelles to Homer, and the remarkable costume and venerable beard and wizened eyes of the older contemplating figure seem more appropriate to the ancient philosopher than to the artist. Moreover, Apelles was young and virile enough to be given the emperor's mistress Campaspe as a gift from his patron, according to Pliny, in return for portraying her nude, so that story fails completely to correspond to the figure seen in the painting.

Rembrandt's self-image concerning his roles as an artist, real and fanciful, shifted frequently across the course of his career but remained an ongoing preoccupation. As noted above, he misleadingly included gold chains in some early, ambitious painted self-portraits – an assertion of status that would continue into the 1640s. Self-portraits appear in all three media: paintings, etchings and (less frequently) drawings. In total Rembrandt produced fully 85 self-portraits. At the outset of his career, particularly while working in his newly acquired medium of etching, Rembrandt used himself as his main model, frequently making experimental small-scale self-portraits, often with exaggerated facial expressions to convey the passions or momentary emotions, such as surprise, disgust, suffering or delight. In a few early impressions of those etchings, Rembrandt would draw over his print with black chalk to enhance and control the effects of shading. A few etchings with self-portraits also show additional figure studies, such as beggars, in other portions of their copper-plate matrix. A number of early paintings and etchings, many of them pure head studies, or *tronies*, also experiment boldly with lighting, placing his eyes in deep shadow.

As we have seen with the early painted Passion pictures (one of which is *Descent from the Cross*, 1633; see illus. 27), produced for stadholder Frederik Hendrik, Rembrandt deliberately inserted his own likeness as a bystander, witness or even accomplice in religious scenes; indeed, his very earliest religious painting, the *Stoning of St Stephen* (1625), already shows him among the observers and tormentors of the saint. Soon after his move to Amsterdam, Rembrandt began to experiment with costume in both paintings and prints, doffing old-fashioned costume of the previous century, especially berets or velvet caps with plumes, sometimes with embroidered cloaks. He even sports a crown and kris-like sabre in one etching (1634; B. 18), and in one early painting (1631) he appears at full-length in 'oriental costume', complete with cloak, satin kaftan and plumed turban, while sporting a walking-stick and a pet poodle at his feet.

In his very largest self-portrait (1658) Rembrandt still maintains this image of a potentate, now frontally enthroned with a silver-tipped stick – at once both a maulstick and a cane but functioning as a sceptre-like attribute. He still wears his (by-then) signature beret but also a sixteenth-century fur-trimmed scholarly tabard cloak over his broadly painted gold jerkin with red sash. The late-style, broadly executed brush-work exemplifies his mature handling, seemingly alluding to the bravura precedents of Titian and Anthony van Dyck, whose unusual but distinctive seated portrait of confident fellow artist Maarten Ryckaert (*c.* 1631) could have been a model for Rembrandt, based on van Dyck's own print after it.

Costume in his self-portraits seems to have been a major opportunity for posing and role-playing for Rembrandt. Among his favoured costume elements, in many early portraits and figure studies as well as painted self-portraits, is a neck armour piece or gorget. Worn by military officers, this segment of practical military armour conferred on the sitter by implication – Rembrandt included – an aura of bravery and patriotic engagement with the recent heroic past of the Dutch Revolt – the same virtues that the militia company would embody in the artist's later *Nightwatch* group portrait (1642).

Far bolder, but also self-deprecating as role-playing in Rembrandt's early work is his self-portrait with his young bride Saskia as the *Prodigal Son in the Tavern* (c. 1635; illus. 53). Here his physiognomic studies bear fruit in the grinning but also drunken features of this overdressed young man with plumed beret and sword, who holds on his lap a tavern wench. Both figures wear costumes from the previous century. He raises a tall glass of beer with his free hand; an expensive stuffed game pie sits on the table before the couple. Notwithstanding the portraits, which were recognized by early collectors, this dissipation recounts the New Testament parable of the Prodigal Son (Luke 15:11–32), which tells of a profligate son who squanders his patrimony on women, gambling and drink in taverns. Of course, in 1634 when he painted himself in this guise, Rembrandt was at the height of his fame and fortune, the most fashionable portraitist in prosperous Amsterdam and a happily married newlywed. While he inserts himself into a biblical story, in this case he is no longer an Everyman among the followers or tormentors of Christ in the Passion; instead, he is an individual, fully conscious of how this depicted story of decadence and sinfulness will end up. Yet for all his self-awareness and well-placed warning in paint against his own profligacy, Rembrandt would soon (in 1639) buy the expensive house on Breestraat, taking on a financial burden that would be his undoing in less than two decades.

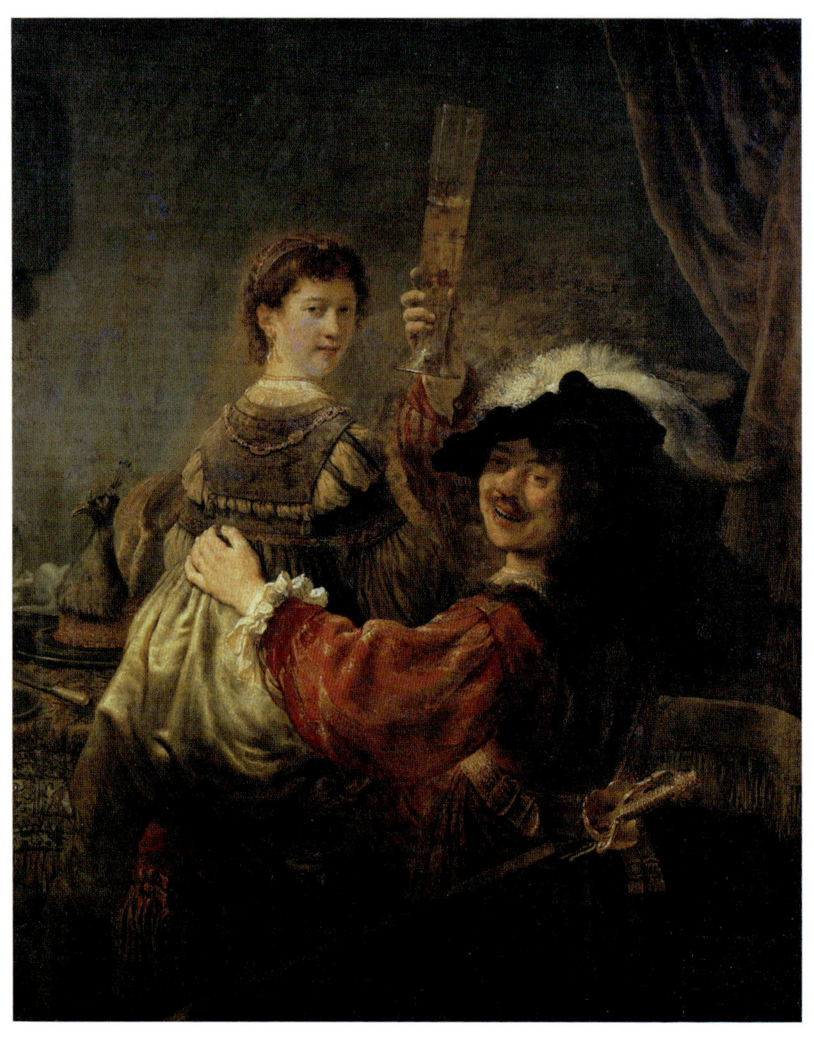

53 Rembrandt, *Prodigal Son in the Tavern (Self-portrait with Saskia)*, c. 1635, oil on canvas.

Meanwhile, one year later, the artist etched another double portrait with his wife, both still in fancy, old-fashioned garb (1636; B. 19). This time Rembrandt shows himself as a working artist, eyes in shadow, holding an etching needle or pen, while Saskia looks on over his shoulder. This time she may assume the role of either model or muse.

Soon afterwards, however, Rembrandt chose to represent himself with all the elegance of a titled gentleman. In both an etching of 1639 (B. 21; illus. 54) and a painting of 1640, he turns from resting his arm casually on a stone sill to face the viewer and assert his superior status. While the frontal face and turned body continue the pose of the double portrait etching with Saskia, here Rembrandt's assertion of both arm and sleeve above a ledge closely derives from his recent experience of the Titian portrait owned by Alphonso Lopez; his repose also derives from Raphael's celebrated portrait of a sophisticated courtier, *Baldassare Castiglione*. Once more the fashion is sixteenth century and shows costly fur trim; particularly in the etching, the grooming of his hair and face echo courtly van Dyck sitters, known from prints. Rembrandt's own recent students, particularly Ferdinand Bol and Govaert Flinck, rapidly adopted this same pictorial formula for their own confident self-portraits, and Rembrandt would reprise it himself for one of his most aristocratic painted portraits, *Nicolaes Bambeek* (1641). This kind of derivation from canonical models certainly confirms the international awareness and professional ambition of Rembrandt around the apogee of his success and the purchase of his lordly home in 1639.

In contrast, Rembrandt also quite willingly portrayed himself as a working craftsman of his artist's trade. The most

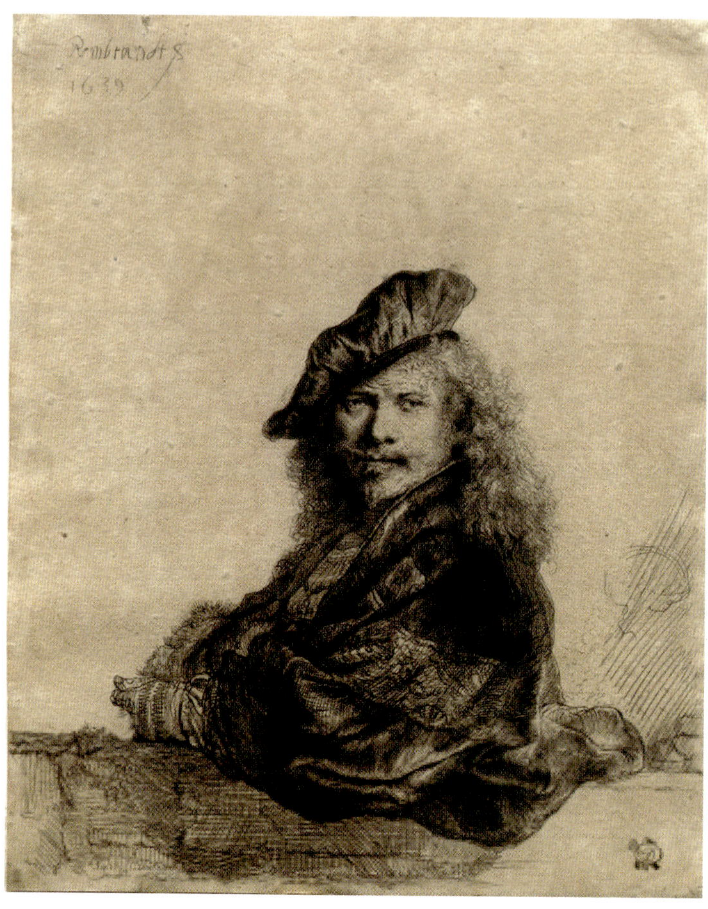

striking of these depictions is his 1648 etching *Self-portrait at a Window* (B. 22; illus. 55). This return to a self-portrait print came in the wake of a number of personal setbacks: particularly the death of Saskia in 1642 as well as of two infants and his mother, the gradual but intense falling-out with nurse-maid Geertje Dirckx and increasing financial difficulties. Instead of a jaunty cap with feather, Rembrandt wears a

54 Rembrandt, *Self-portrait Leaning on a Stone Sill*, 1639, etching.

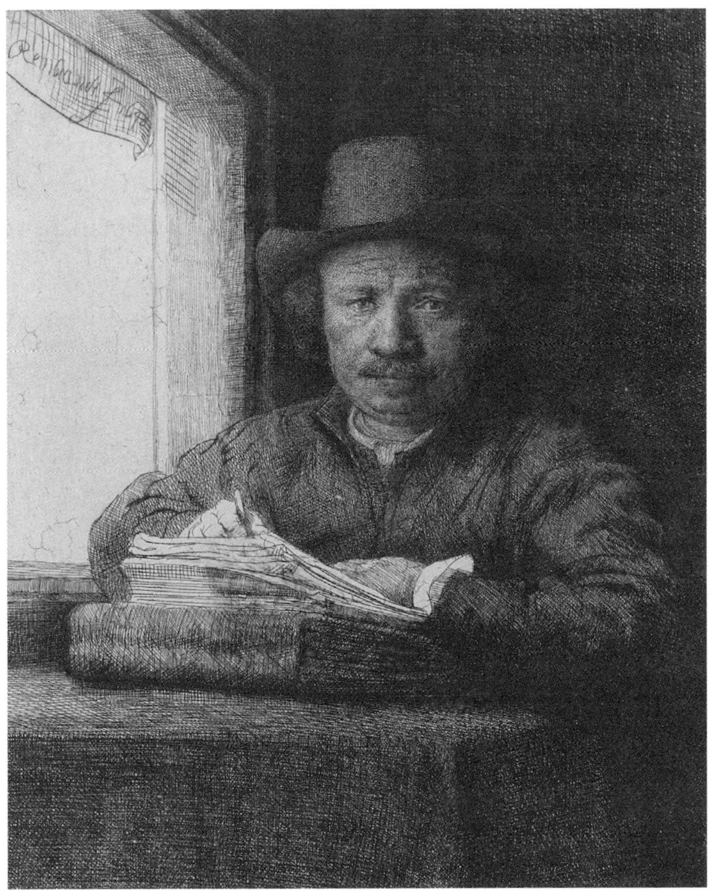

simple dark hat and coat and sits quietly at a table, working at
a lectern in a dark chamber from the natural light of an open
window, which reveals a hilly landscape background. Again,
his tool could be either an etching needle or a pen, but his
assignment is a humbler work on paper rather than a painting
– this in a decade in which very few major paintings were
produced after the *Nightwatch*. Despite signs of ageing in a

55 Rembrandt, *Self-portrait at a Window*, 1648, etching.

puffier face with jowls, his gaze outwards from the shadows is frank and steady, absorbed in observation. Of course, in Italian art theory, mastery of draughtsmanship was a cardinal virtue of the serious artist, but here Rembrandt does not seem to be asserting either mastery or status; indeed, the book on which his work rests is used as a support rather than an attribute of erudition.

Another life-sized painted portrait shows work clothes – a smock and cap alone – without other attributes (1652). It presents a dark brown harmony with only the older, furrowed face illuminated; the painter stands in an informal yet confident frontal pose with arms akimbo, both thumbs resting on his sash. The artist also made a similar small self-portrait drawing at full length, posed with similar relaxed hands and extended elbows while dressed in his work clothes (*c.* 1650; Amsterdam, Rembrandt House), possibly as a study for the large Vienna image. These humbler self-representations were followed by one more massive, frontal half-length painting from his final decade, showing the artist as a painter at work: *Self-portrait with Palette* (*c.* 1665; illus. 56). Again the painter frankly depicts his features, now significantly older, with grey hair, sagging flesh and even more wrinkles, harshly lighted from the side with strong cast shadows. His clothing includes a painter's cap, although his fur-trimmed robe and jerkin echo the massive Frick potentate image of mastery. This time, Rembrandt holds the tools of his painting trade. Broadly painted, a cluster of brushes and a palette as well as a protruding maulstick dissolve into what would be his left hand, suggesting the messiness of pigment as well as virtuoso brushwork for its own sake. His posture of extended elbows in his dark robe here adds a strong pyramidal solidity to the layout, as the white cap and shirt frame his face with bright episodes.

No clear studio space is depicted in the background, but two large perfect half-circles adorn the wall behind the painter to reassert its surface behind him. Those circles almost certainly capture part of the standard two-hemisphere layout of contemporary large Dutch wall maps, which in turn suggests how much the steady gaze of this artist encompasses. Such confidently steady, unbroken curves may also refer to the legend of the great founding painter of the Italian Renaissance, Giotto, whose freehand circles first signalled his prodigious early talent as a virtuoso. The actual canvas on the easel is only barely visible at the upper right edge of the Kenwood image. The image even openly admits to being a painting made directly from a mirror reflection, since now the right-handed painter, with one hand again on his hip, holds his tools in his left hand instead.

Thus in contrast to the tiny but assertive panel the early *Painter in the Studio* (see illus. 3), which might well be a self-portrait and stages a confrontation between the artist and his easel, this revealing late Kenwood self-portrait exudes maturity, mastery and professionalism without either emotion or drama. In that respect, its bold yet assured brushwork shows the distance and confidence acquired across a lifetime of experience. While the late work still remains reflexive, its studio setting stands worlds away from the meticulous verisimilitude of the ambitious beginner.

During 1669, the last year of his life, Rembrandt would still paint two frank and moving self-portraits that reveal his features, his grey hair, but also his steady gaze and hand.

Amazingly, the late London *Self-portrait* even reprises the half-length pose and calm assurance of the 1640 London *Self-portrait on a Window Sill*. Here our impressions confirm how much continuity of vision and pose unites the two works, whereas the late Hague *Self-portrait* provides a valedictory bust, freely and candidly confronting both age and self-awareness.

Rembrandt's last decade of self-portraits also makes several revealing assertions about his commitments. Clearest of all is his religious declaration in the form of a *portrait historié*, or portrait as a historical character, like his self-portrait as Prodigal Son. In this case the subject is another biblical figure where he melds his own features: the *Self-portrait as Apostle Paul* (1661; illus. 57). The apostle is shown holding an open book, presumably holy Scripture, as he turns to look up from his studies to engage the viewer or respond, perhaps even to share the text for discussion (see illus. 21, here identified as a discussion between SS Peter and Paul). Paul, after all, was also a preacher, so his own sermons and epistles offer commentary on the Bible. The spot of bright light falls on his brow, wrapped in a turban-like headdress. His wrinkled brow and ageing flesh emerge from a complex range of shadows. What expressly marks this particular religious figure as Paul is his personal attribute, the hilt of a sword beneath his left arm, symbol of his martyrdom.

This image of Paul, in turn, conforms to a suite of his paintings from around the same moment, which loosely comprise a series of similar, portrait-like half-lengths of apostles; in the years right after his 1656 bankruptcy Rembrandt was already experimenting with this kind of isolated individual

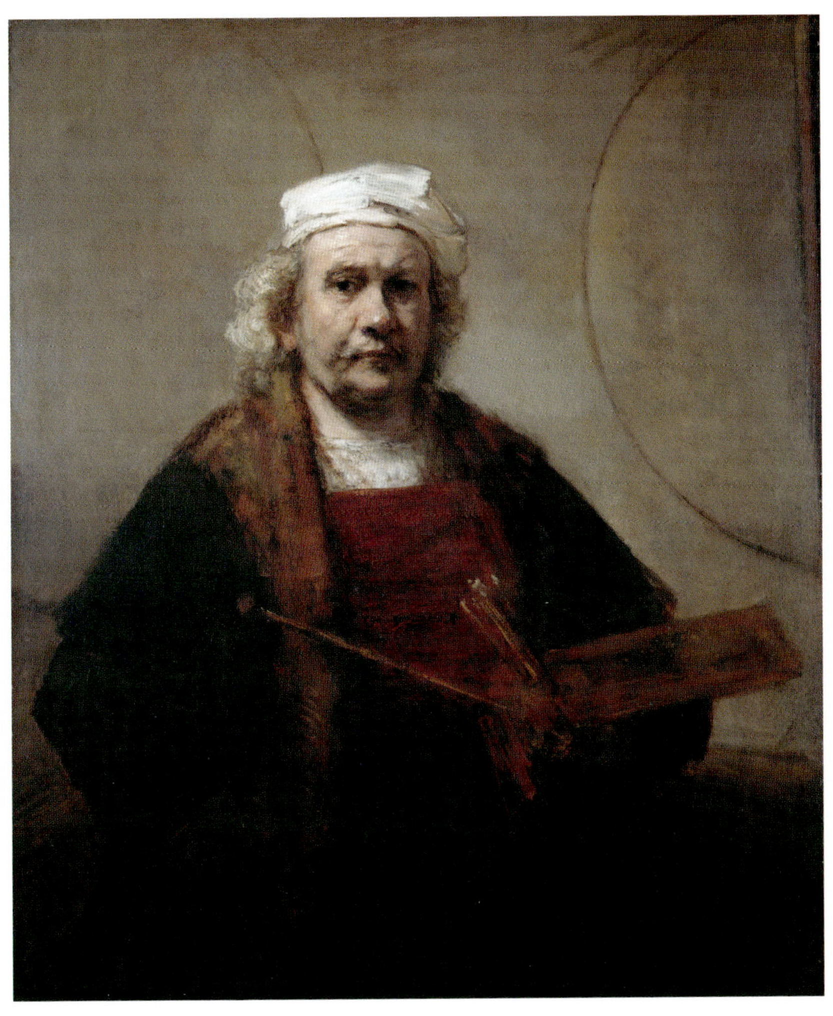

56 Rembrandt, *Self-portrait with Palette, c.* 1665, oil on canvas.

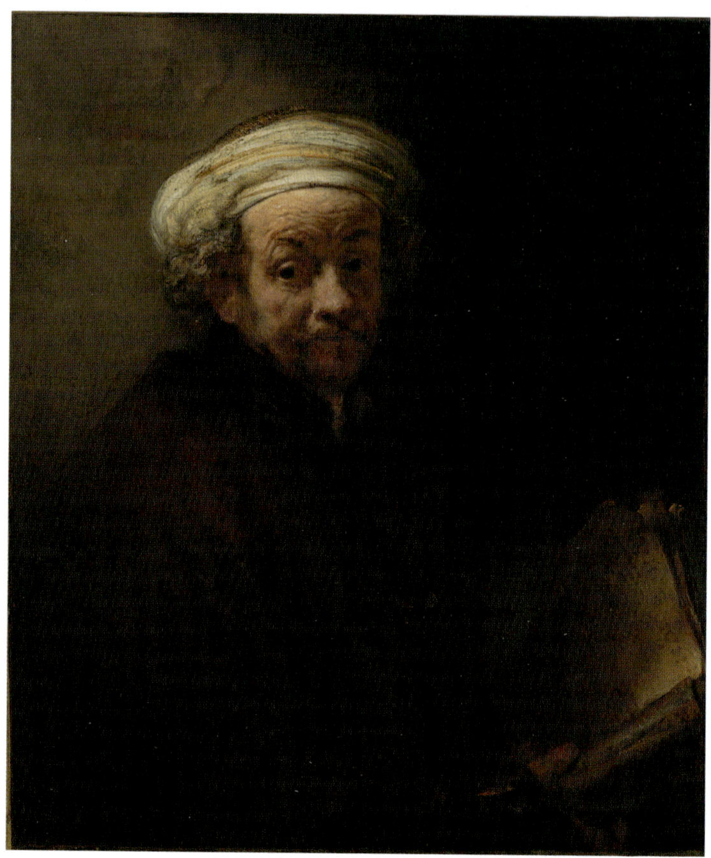

religious figure at half-length, lost in contemplation against
dark backgrounds (for example, *Apostle Paul*, writing at his
desk, *c.* 1657). Other dated works of 1661 also include *Matthew*,
Bartholomew, *Simon* and *James* as well as related half-length
images of the Resurrected Christ, and the Virgin Mary as
Mater Dolorosa. Most are consistently painted with the late
style of broad brushwork and heavy impasto in brown tones;
however, their sizes and degree of finish sometimes vary, so

57 Rembrandt, *Self-portrait as Apostle Paul*, 1661, oil on canvas.

this project does not seem conceived expressly as a series for display together, in contrast to numerous print series for albums or painted series by both Rubens and van Dyck. Thus, the Rembrandt canvases do not comprise a full, systematic set, and they even vary in terms of information conveyed.

More significant, surely, is Rembrandt's choice of Paul to display his own features. While Paul was not a direct, lifetime disciple of Christ, his posthumous evangelism for the new religion helped define its fundamental tenets, particularly the concept of grace and justification by faith alone. Rembrandt had already painted several images of Paul, including an early *Paul in Prison* (1627) but also more recently an *Elderly Man as St Paul* (165[9?]), itself probably another, unidentified *portrait historié*. Paul held special significance for various Protestant denominations, beginning with Martin Luther but also emphasized by John Calvin and Menno Simons, so his image by Rembrandt does not specifically indicate any individual denomination for the painter. However, Calvin particularly singled out Paul for attention:

> we ought to pay more regard to the apostleship of Paul than to that of Peter, since the Holy Spirit, in allotting them different provinces, destined Peter for the Jews and Paul for us. (*Institutes of the Christian Religion* IV: 6, 15)

Rembrandt's specific creed is notoriously difficult to determine, but his pictures align with Calvin's teachings, especially regarding the Old Testament covenant, and surely his art reaffirms his Christian commitment, reinforced in this image of his *Self-portrait as Paul*. And like the inscriptions on engraved portraits by Albrecht Dürer and Lucas Cranach of Protestant leaders in sixteenth-century Germany, such as Martin Luther or his lieutenant Philipp Melanchthon, the face stands in for the writings and theological thought: 'Dürer was able to depict Philipp's features as if living, but the skilled hand could not portray his soul'; or, 'Luther himself gave form to an eternal likeness of his spirit; Lucas portrayed the mortal appearance.' Rembrandt, however, goes further, literally identifying himself with his chosen saint, and his sword, held close to the heart, can be understood through the words of Paul as 'the sword of the Spirit, which is the Word of God' (Ephesians 6:17).

One other late self-portrait at bust length, very broadly brushed, also shows an aged Rembrandt turning to face the viewer but with a ridiculous grin on his face (*c.* 1663; illus. 58). Although this canvas has been cut down on all sides and has darkened and yellowed, some of its main features remain clear. The beret-topped painter is at work here, maulstick in hand, and he turns away from a dour half-length image on his canvas. Earlier interpretations saw that contrast between the smiling painter and his sombre sitter as an antithesis, akin to the classical motif of two ancient philosophers – Democritus, who could only laugh at the follies of the world, and Heraclitus, who wept over them.

But a larger painting (1685) by Rembrandt's final pupil, Aert de Gelder, reveals the true subject of this mysterious painting that is given Rembrandt's own features. In fact, De Gelder's work presents a classical painter: Zeuxis, most famous for the story in Pliny that he assembled five beautiful women in order to paint an image of Helen of Troy by selecting the

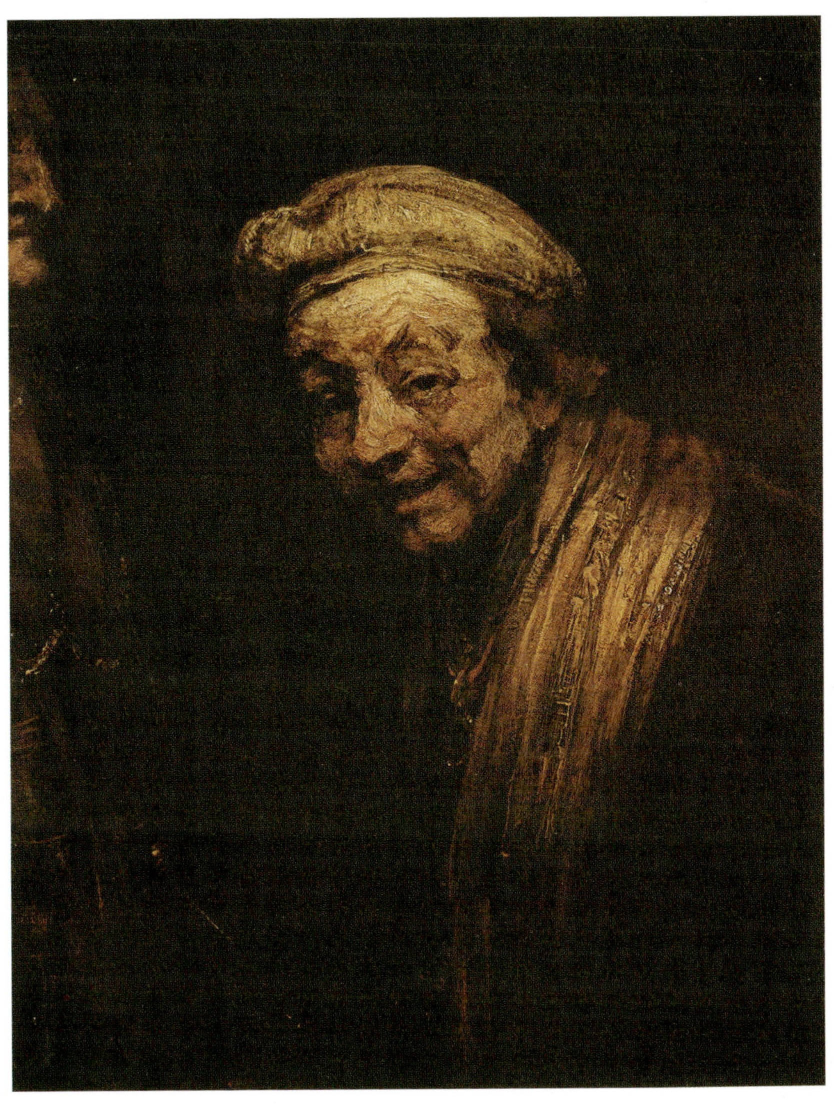

58 Rembrandt, *Self-portrait, Grinning, c.* 1663, oil on canvas.

best features of each. Zeuxis also legendarily could paint grapes so lifelike that birds would fly up to eat them. In De Gelder's picture, by contrast, the painter has a studiously unattractive woman posing for her portrait. Albert Blankert connected the two images together through a common Zeuxis story, repeated by Karel van Mander in the appendix to his 1604 *Schilderboek* and later by Rembrandt's former pupil, painter-theorist Samuel van Hoogstraten, in his book, *Inleyding tot de hooge schoole der schilderkonst* (Introduction to the Art of Painting, 1678). As an old man, Zeuxis, by this account, literally died laughing while making the portrait of a 'wrinkled, droll old woman'. In De Gelder's large painting, the younger painter, then aged forty, appended his own features, turning outward to share the laugh with the viewer. This pose lends further credence to its association with the Cologne self-portrait of the laughing Rembrandt, now also as an aged Zeuxis, standing before the portrait on the easel of another ugly figure, who turns out to be an unsmiling woman. X-rays reveal that originally he painted his left hand with a brush, actively painting that portrait.

With this ironic act of self-depiction, Rembrandt casts a sceptical eye on his entire career as a portrait painter at the lifelong service of clients, including portraits made during his financially straitened circumstances in the final decade and a half of his career. Another irony: among his latest clients was Gerard de Lairesse, the future arch-classicist and representative of an antithetical aesthetic to Rembrandt, whose own face was disfigured by a bridgeless nose, possibly the result of congenital syphilis (1665). How typical of Rembrandt to be both learned and irreverent, even when aligning himself with a classical story of art-making, specifically with Zeuxis, normally famous for his painting of Helen, the paragon of beauty.

Thus the Cologne painting is a self-portrait that reveals artistic identity all the more vividly – a desire to use tradition, even to assimilate into it, but also to retain an irreverent last laugh, here combining the mundane, even the foolish, with the classical. Even at the height of his ambitious first decade in Amsterdam, Rembrandt still could make Rubens's spiritual athlete of Christ into a humble, fleshly corpse in his own *Descent from the Cross* or, later, a portrait-like *tronie*. Rembrandt could freely mix pictorial genres or stamp all his work with the irrepressible mark of ordinary, if vital humans.

In this respect, for all his self-conscious ambitions to absorb and emulate the examples of Titian and Rubens and to join the ranks of venerated old master painters in art history, Rembrandt still belongs to his seventeenth-century Dutch surroundings. We can readily compare his late Cologne *Self-portrait, Grinning* to an earlier self-portrait (*c.* 1630; illus. 59) by his most acclaimed contemporary woman artist, Judith Leyster of Haarlem (1609–1660). Rather than wearing work clothes, like the later Rembrandt, she is fashionably dressed in lace collar and cap but she wears boldly coloured sleeves and skirt, as if the subject of her own careful portrait-making. Yet she sits at ease, smiling confidently as she holds brush and palette in her hands, pausing in the very process of painting a canvas of her own. Her subject is one of her signature figures, a genre character of a merry fiddler wearing the baggy stock slapstick costume of contemporary *commedia dell'arte* clowns, dancers and merrymakers more familiar from French prints and paintings. Her own broad brushwork stems

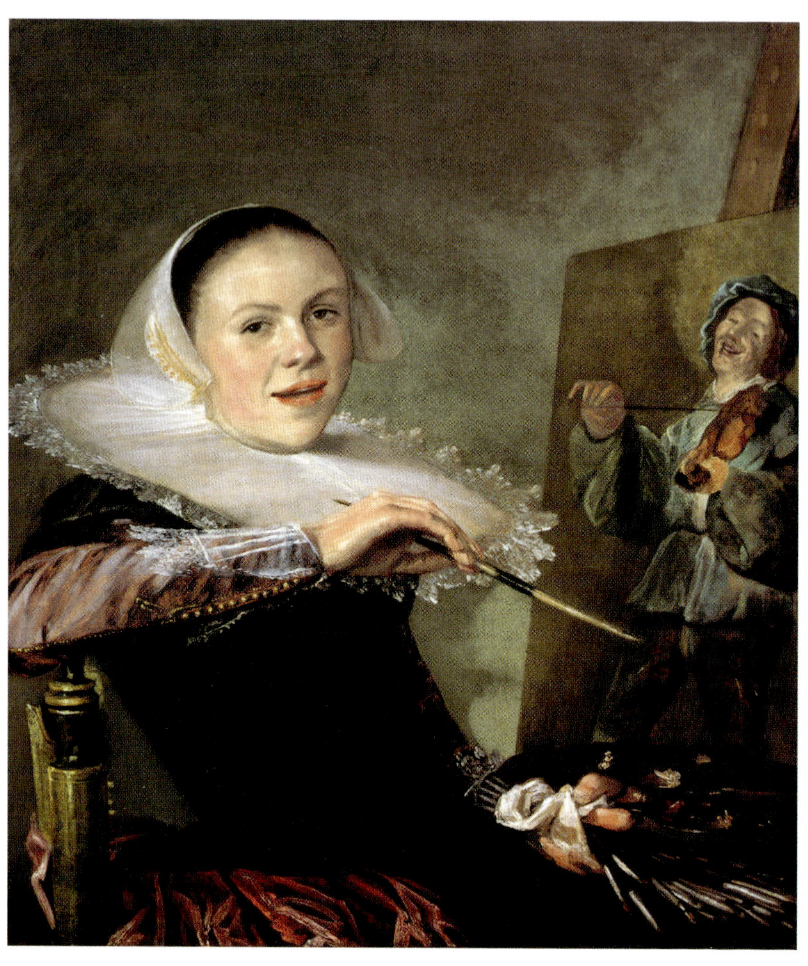

59 Judith Leyster, *Self-portrait at an Easel, c.* 1630, oil on canvas.

from the dazzling bravura of her teacher Frans Hals, who also painted comic genre figures as well as portraits. (X-rays reveal that before the fiddler a portrait of a woman sat on Leyster's easel.) Even the pose of a figure leaning back and turning in a chair derives from several Hals portraits, for all its seeming naturalness.

Unlike Leyster and many of his other Dutch contemporaries who specialized in such works, Rembrandt seldom painted genre pictures, although his drawings and prints include vignettes of both daily life and foolish behaviour by adults and children – even beggars. His own life, especially his house and his large collection, suggests more serious ambitions, which also appear in his career choices, especially to give uncharacteristic attention in Holland to biblical subjects. Rembrandt's overall emphasis remains on the human figure in a serious mood – sometimes both serious and biblical, as in the moral dilemmas of his *Bathsheba* or *Denial of Peter*. Over time, Rembrandt becomes increasingly engaged with thoughtful or absorbed individuals, lost in thought or listening. He gives up dramatic, gestural action and close description for evocative dark lighting and quiet, still isolation. In his self-portraits, he increasingly opts for a kind of studied awkwardness in both facture and pose, largely abandoning his pretence to gentility and status for frank engagement as a craftsman with his viewer. Yet he never abandons a willingness to link to a world of serious spirituality (*Self-portrait as Paul*) as a major component of his wider interests, even while acknowledging a comic side to learned classicism (*Self-portrait, Grinning*). Perhaps torn, like *Aristotle*, between worldliness and creative interiority, he will opt, like *Homer*, for insight rather than pure sight. Ultimately he hopes, like the Prodigal Son, for forgiveness of sins, even those recorded in the double portrait amid his own early profligacy (*Prodigal Son in the Tavern*), but finally achieved (*Return of the Prodigal Son*, c. 1669) in the utter humiliation of his final years.

For that representation of the human in all its aspects, we continually return to the enduring art of Rembrandt van Rijn.

CHRONOLOGY

1606	Birth of Rembrandt Harmenszoon van Rijn in Leiden on 15 July
c. 1618–20	Attends Latin School in Leiden
1620	Registers at Leiden University
c. 1621–4	Pupil of Jacob van Swanenburg in Leiden
c. 1624	Pupil of Pieter Lastman in Amsterdam
1625	First dated painting: *Stoning of St Stephen* (Lyons)
c. 1628–31	First pupils in Leiden: Gerard Dou and Isack Jouderville. Close association in Leiden with Jan Lievens
1629	Favourable critical reception by Constantijn Huygens, secretary of stadholder Frederik Hendrik. *Judas Returning the Thirty Pieces of Silver* (private collection, UK)
1632	Lodges in Amsterdam with dealer Hendrick Uylenburgh. *Anatomy Lesson of Dr Nicholas Tulp* (The Hague); portrait of Amalia van Solms and start of Passion series for her husband, stadholder Frederik Hendrik: *Raising of the Cross* and *Descent from the Cross* (both Munich)
1633	Painted and etched portraits of Remonstrant leader Johann Uytenbogaert
1634	Marriage to Saskia Uylenburgh. Becomes member of Amsterdam guild of St Luke
c. 1634–5	Govaert Flinck becomes pupil
1635	Rembrandt leaves Uylenburgh studio for independent practice. Flinck succeeds Rembrandt as head of Uylenburgh atelier. Birth of son, Robertus (d. February 1636)

1636	New Passion painting, *Ascension* (Munich) sent to The Hague
c. 1636	Ferdinand Bol becomes pupil
1638, 1640	Two daughters, both named Cornelia, die as infants
1639	Buys home (today Rembrandthuis) on Sint Anthonisbreestraat Two more Passion paintings sent to The Hague: *Entombment* and *Resurrection* (both Munich)
1640	Samuel van Hoogstraten becomes pupil (later author of major art theory treatise, *Inleyding tot de Hooge Schoole der Schilderkonst, anders de Zichtbare Werelt*, 1678)
1641	Son Titus born (only child of Saskia to survive)
1642	Death of Saskia on 14 June Completion of *Nightwatch* (Amsterdam) Geertje Dirckx hired as nursemaid to Titus and becomes Rembrandt's mistress
1646	Frederik Hendrik pays Rembrandt for two paintings of Infancy of Christ
c. 1647	Hendrickje Stoffels, live-in servant, becomes common-law wife of Rembrandt
1649	Geertje Dirckx sues Rembrandt for breach of marriage promise and receives an annual allowance
1650	Geertje Dirckx committed to women's home of correction, Gouda
1652	Dated drawings for *album amicorum* of Jan Six
1654	Hendrickje Stoffels summoned and denied communion by Reformed Church Daughter Cornelia born out of wedlock
1656	Rembrandt files for bankruptcy (*cessio bonorum*), draws up inventory for auction *Anatomy Lesson of Dr Deyman* (fragment; Amsterdam)
1658	Moves to rented house in Jordaan section of Amsterdam
1660	Creation of dealership with Rembrandt employed by Titus and Hendrickje Stoffels
c. 1660	Aert de Gelder becomes final pupil
1661	*Oath of Claudius Civilis*, painted decoration of Amsterdam Town Hall (fragment; Stockholm)

1662	*Syndics of the Drapers' Guild* (Amsterdam)
1663	Death of Hendrickje Stoffels in July
1668	Titus marries Magdalena van Loo in February
	Titus dies on 7 September
1669	Death of Rembrandt on 4 October; buried in Westerkerk, Amsterdam

Major Dates in Dutch History

1568–1648	Beginning of Dutch Revolt: war for independence from Spanish royal rule
1575	Foundation of Leiden University after unsuccessful Spanish siege of city
1579	Union of Utrecht, establishing federation of northern provinces of Netherlands, the Dutch Republic
1582/3	Birth of Frans Hals (d. 1666)
1584	Assassination of William I of Orange ('the Silent'), leader of Dutch Revolt; succeeded as stadholder by son Maurits of Nassau
1602	Foundation of Dutch East Indies Company (VOC)
1609–21	Truce with Spain, de facto recognition of Dutch Republic by Spain
1613–62	Expansion of Amsterdam with new rings of canals
1618–19	Synod of Dort (Dordrecht) by Dutch Reformed Church
	Hugo Grotius flees Netherlands for exile in France
1619	Trial and execution of Advocate Johan van Oldenbarnevelt
	Suppression of Remonstrants by Counter-Remonstrants of Reformed Church
	Dutch foundation of East Indies capital at Batavia in Java
1621	War resumes with Spain
	Foundation of Dutch West Indies Company (WIC)
1625	Foundation of New Amsterdam on Manhattan Island (modern-day New York)
	Death of Maurits of Nassau; succeeded as stadholder by younger brother, Frederik Hendrik
	Johan Uytenbogaert returns from religious exile to The Hague

1629–54	Dutch occupation of Brazil, former colony of Portugal
1637	Publication of Dutch States Bible
1639–45	Decoration of Militia Company Hall (Kloveniersdoelen) with group portraits
1640	Death of Peter Paul Rubens (b. 1577)
1641	Marriage of son of Frederik Hendrik, William (II), to Mary Stuart of England
1647	Death of Frederik Hendrik and succession by William II
1648	Peace of Westphalia and official recognition of Dutch Republic
1648–55	Construction of new Amsterdam Town Hall by Jacob van Campen
1650	William II attempts to capture Amsterdam, dies; birth of son, future William III
1650–72	'Stadholderless' period
1652–4	First Anglo-Dutch War
1655	Rabbi Menasseh ben Israel publishes *Piedra gloriosa* with Rembrandt etchings
1655–97	Decoration of Amsterdam Town Hall with paintings by Govaert Flinck, Ferdinand Bol, Jan Lievens
1660	Death of Govaert Flinck and interruption of paintings for Amsterdam Town Hall
1662	*Atlas major* published in Amsterdam by Joan Blaeu
1664	English seize New Amsterdam and rename it New York
1665–7	Second Anglo-Dutch War
1672	Invasion of Netherlands by Louis XIV of France
1672–4	Third Anglo-Dutch War
1677	Marriage of William III to Mary Stuart, daughter of James II of England
1688	William sails to intervene in England; Bloodless Revolution

BIBLIOGRAPHY

Ackley, Clifford, *Rembrandt's Journey*, exh. cat., Boston, Museum of Fine Arts (Boston, MA, 2003)

Adams, Ann Jensen, *Public Faces and Private Identities in Seventeenth-century Holland: Portraiture and the Production of Community* (Cambridge, 2009)

—, ed., *Rembrandt's 'Bathsheba Reading King David's Letter'* (Cambridge, 1998)

Alexander-Knotter, Mirjam, Jasper Hillegers and Edward van Voolen, *The 'Jewish' Rembrandt: The Myth Unravelled*, exh. cat. (Amsterdam, 2008)

Baer, Ronni, *Class Distinctions: Dutch Painting in the Age of Rembrandt and Vermeer*, exh. cat., Boston, Museum of Fine Arts (Boston, MA, 2015)

Bailey, Anthony, *Rembrandt's House* (New York, 1978)

Berger, Harry, Jr, *Manhood, Marriage, and Mischief: Rembrandt's 'Night Watch' and Other Dutch Group Portraits* (New York, 2007)

Bergvelt, Ellinoor, and Renée Kistemaker, *De Wereld binnen Handbereik: Nederlandse Kunst- en Rariteitenverzamelingen, 1585–1735*, exh. cat., Amsterdam, Historical Museum (Amsterdam, 1992)

Bikker, Jonathan, Gregor Weber, Marjorie Wieseman and Erik Hinterding, *Rembrandt The Late Works*, exh. cat., London, National Gallery, and Amsterdam, Rijksmuseum (London and Amsterdam, 2014)

Blankert, Albert, et al., *Dutch Classicism*, exh. cat., Rotterdam, Museum Boijmans van Beuningen; Frankfurt, Staedel Boogert; Amsterdam, Rembrandt House (Rotterdam and Frankfurt, 2000)

Boogaart, Ernst van den, *Civil and Corrupt Asia: Image and Text in the 'Itinerario' and the 'Icones' of Jan Huygen van Linschoten* (Chicago, IL, 2003)

—, ed., *Johan Maurits van Nassau-Siegen 1604–1679* (The Hague, 1979)

Boogert, Bob van den, ed., *Rembrandt's Treasures*, exh. cat. (Amsterdam, 1999)

Brienen, Rebecca Parker, 'Embodying Race and Pleasure: Dirck Valkenburg's *Slave Dance*', *Nederlands Kunsthistorisch Jaarboek*, LVIII (2007–8), pp. 265–87

—, *Visions of Savage Paradise: Albert Eckhout, Court Painter in Colonial Dutch Brazil* (Amsterdam, 2006)

Brotton, Jerry, *A History of the World in Twelve Maps* (New York, 2012), pp. 218–93

Carasso-Kok, M., and J. Levy-van Halm, eds, *Schutters in Holland: Kracht en Zenuwen van de Stad* (Zwolle, 1988)

Carroll, Margaret, 'Accidents Will Happen: The Case of *The Nightwatch*', in *Rethinking Rembrandt*, ed. Alan Chong and Michael Zell (Boston, MA, 2002), pp. 91–105

—, 'Civic Ideology and Its Subversion: Rembrandt's *Oath of Claudius Civilis*', *Art History*, IX (1986), pp. 12–35

—, 'Rembrandt as Meditational Printmaker', *Art Bulletin*, LXIII (1981), pp. 587–610

—, 'Rembrandt's *Nightwatch* and the Iconological Tradition of Militia Portraiture in Amsterdam', PhD thesis, Harvard University, Cambridge, MA (1976)

Chapman, H. Perry, *Rembrandt's Self-portraits: A Study in Seventeenth-century Identity* (Princeton, NJ, 1990)

Chong, Alan, ed., *Rembrandt Creates Rembrandt: Art and Ambition in Leiden, 1629–1631* (Zwolle, 2000)

Coelen, Peter van der, *Patriarchs, Angels, and Prophets: The Old Testament in Netherlandish Printmaking from Lucas van Leyden to Rembrandt*, exh. cat., Amsterdam, Rembrandt House; Rotterdam, Museum Boijmans van Beuningen (Amsterdam, 1996)

—, *Rembrandts Passie*, exh. cat. (Rotterdam, 2006)

Cook, Harold, *Matters of Exchange: Commerce, Medicine, and Science in the Dutch Golden Age* (New Haven, CT, 2007)

Corrêa do Lago, Pedro, and Bia Corrêa do Lago, *Frans Post (1612–1680)* (Milan, 2007)

Crenshaw, Paul, *Rembrandt's Bankruptcy: The Artist, His Patrons, and the Art Market in Seventeenth-century Netherlands* (Cambridge, 2006)

Dewitt, Lloyd, *Rembrandt and the Face of Jesus*, exh. cat., Philadelphia
    Museum of Art (Philadelphia, PA, 2011)
Dickey, Stephanie, *Rembrandt: Portraits in Print* (Amsterdam, 2004)
Duerloo, Luc, and R. Malcolm Smuts, eds, *The Age of Rubens: Diplomacy,
    Dynastic Politics and the Visual Arts in Early Seventeenth-century Europe*
    (Turnhout, 2016)
Emmens, J. A., *Rembrandt en de Regels van de Kunst* [1964] (Amsterdam, 1979)
Filipczak, Zirka Zaremba, 'Rembrandt and the Body Language
    of Mughal Miniatures', *Nederlands Kunsthistorisch Jaarboek*, LVIII
    (2007), pp. 162–87
Ford, Charles, 'Rembrandt's Self-portraits as a Category', in *Rethinking
    Rembrandt*, ed. Alan Chong and Michael Zell (Boston, MA, 2002),
    pp. 121–7
Fremantle, Katherine, *The Baroque Town Hall of Amsterdam* (Utrecht, 1959)
Gaastra, Femme, *The Dutch East India Company: Expansion and Decline*
    (Zutphen, 2003)
Gaehtgens, Barbara, 'Rembrandt's *Ganymede*, or the Princely Eagle
    Test', unpublished lecture, Groningen, 2015
Georgievska-Shine, Aneta, and Larry Silver, *Rubens, Velázquez, and the
    King of Spain* (Farnham, 2014)
Golahny, Amy, *Rembrandt's Reading: The Artist's Bookshelf of Ancient Poetry
    and History* (Amsterdam, 2003)
Gyllenhaal, Martha, 'Rembrandt's Artful Use of Statues and Casts:
    New Insights into His Studio Practices and Working Methods',
    PhD thesis, Temple University, Philadelphia (2008)
Haak, Bob, *Rembrandt: His Life, His Work, His Time*, trans. Elizabeth
    Willems-Treeman (New York, 1969)
Halewood, William H., *Six Subjects of Reformation Art: A Preface to
    Rembrandt* (Toronto, 1982)
Haverkamp-Begemann, Egbert, *Rembrandt: The Night Watch*
    (Princeton, NJ, 1982)
Heckscher, William, *Rembrandt's Anatomy of Dr Nicolaas Tulp:
    An Iconological Study* (New York, 1958)
Held, Julius, *Rembrandt's 'Aristotle' and Other Rembrandt Studies*
    (Princeton, NJ, 1969)
Hoffmann, Werner, *Luther und die Folgen für die Kunst* (Hamburg, 1983),
    pp. 309–74

Hommes, Margriet van Eikema, and Elmer Kolfin, *De Oranjezaal in Huis ten Bosch* (Zwolle, 2013)

Israel, Jonathan, *The Dutch Republic: Its Rise, Greatness and Fall, 1477–1806* (Oxford, 1995)

Jardine, Lisa, *Going Dutch: How England Plundered Holland's Glory* (London, 2008)

Kaak, Joachim, *Rembrandts Grisaille 'Johannes der Täufer Predigend': Dekorum-Verstoß oder Ikonographie der Unmoral* (Hildesheim, 1994)

Kaplan, Benjamin, *Divided by Faith: Religious Conflict and the Practice of Toleration in Early Modern Europe* (Cambridge, MA, 2007)

Keblusek, Maria, and Jori Zijlmans, eds, *Princely Display: The Court of Frederik Hendrik of Orange and Amalia van Solms* (The Hague, 1997)

Kempers, Bram, 'Allegory and Symbolism in Rembrandt's *De eendracht van het land*: Images of Concord and Discord in Prints, Medals and Paintings', in *1648. Paix de Westphalie: l'art entre la guerre et la paix. Actes*, ed. Jacques Thuillier and Klaus Bussmann (Paris and Münster, 2000), pp. 71–113

Keyes, George, Tom Rassieur, and Dennis Weller, *Rembrandt in America: Collecting and Connoisseurship* (New York, 2011), esp. pp. 113–39

Kistemaker, Renée, and Roelof van Gelder, *Amsterdam: The Golden Age, 1275–1795*, trans. Paul Foulkes (New York, 1983)

Kok, Erna, 'Culturele Ondernemers in de Gouden Eeuw', PhD thesis, University of Amsterdam (2013)

Lammertse, Friso, and Jaap van der Veen, *Uylenburgh & Son: Art and Commerce from Rembrandt to De Lairesse, 1625–1675*, exh. cat., Amsterdam, Rembrandthuis (Amsterdam, 2006)

Lamster, Mark, *Master of Shadows: The Secret Diplomatic Career of the Painter Peter Paul Rubens* (New York, 2009)

McGrath, Elizabeth, and Jean Michel Massing, eds, *The Slave in European Art: From Renaissance Trophy to Abolitionist Emblem* (London, 2012)

Massing, Jean Michel, *The Image of the Black in Western Art*, vol. III, part 2: *From the 'Age of Discovery' to the Age of Abolition* (Cambridge, MA, 2011), esp. pp. 77–116, 143–82

Mosby, Dewey, ed., *Gods, Saints and Heroes: Dutch Painting in the Age of Rembrandt*, exh. cat., Washington, National Gallery of Art (Washington DC, 1980)

Müller, Jürgen, *Der sokratische Künstler: Studien zu Rembrandts 'Nachtwache'* (Leiden, 2015)

Nadler, Steven, *Rembrandt's Jews* (Chicago, IL, 2003)

Parker, Geoffrey, *The Dutch Revolt* (Ithaca, NY, 1977)

—, *The Military Revolution: Military Innovation and the Rise of the West, 1500–1800* (Cambridge, 1988)

Perlove, Shelley, and Larry Silver, *Rembrandt's Faith: Church and Temple in the Dutch Golden Age* (University Park, PA, 2009)

Ploeg, Peter van der, and Carola Vermeeren, eds, *Princely Patrons: The Court of Frederik Hendrik of Orange and Amalia van Solms in The Hague* (The Hague, 1997)

Prak, Maarten, *The Dutch Republic in the Seventeenth Century: The Golden Age*, trans. Diane Webb (Cambridge, 2005)

Price, J. L., *Dutch Culture in the Golden Age* (London, 2011)

Riegl, Alois, *The Group Portraiture of Holland*, trans. Evelyn Kain (Los Angeles, CA, 1999)

Roodenburg, Herman, *The Eloquence of the Body: Perspectives on Gesture in the Early Dutch Republic* (Zwolle, 2004)

Rosenberg, Charles, *Rembrandt's Religious Prints: The Feddersen Collection at the Snite Museum of Art*, exh. cat., South Bend, Snite Museum (South Bend, IN, 2017)

Rosenberg, Jakob, *Rembrandt: Life and Work* (London, 1964)

Russell, Margareta, 'The Iconography of Rembrandt's *Rape of Ganymede*', *Simiolus*, IX (1977), pp. 5–18

Saslow, James, *Ganymede in the Renaissance: Homosexuality in Art and Society* (New Haven, CT, 1986)

Schama, Simon, *Rembrandt's Eyes* (New York, 1999)

Scheller, R. W., 'Rembrandt en de Encyclopedische Verzameling', *Oud Holland*, LXXXIV (1969), pp. 81–147

Schmidt, Benjamin, *Inventing Exoticism: Geography, Globalism, and Europe's Early Modern World* (Philadelphia, PA, 2015)

Schneider, Cynthia, *Rembrandt's Landscapes: Drawings and Prints* (Washington, DC, 1990)

Scholten, Frits, *Sumptuous Memories: Studies in Seventeenth-century Dutch Tomb Sculpture* (Zwolle, 2003)

Schwartz, Gary, *The Nightwatch* (Amsterdam, 2002)

—, *The Rembrandt Book* (New York, 2006)

—, *Rembrandt: His Life, His Paintings* (New York, 1985)

Slive, Seymour, *Frans Hals* (London, 2014)

—, *Rembrandt and His Critics, 1630–1730* (The Hague, 1953)

—, *Rembrandt Drawings* (Los Angeles, CA, 2009)

Sluijter, Eric Jan, *Rembrandt and the Female Nude* (Amsterdam, 2006)

—, *Rembrandt's Rivals: History Painting in Amsterdam, 1630–1650* (Amsterdam, 2015)

—, et al., eds, *Leidse Fijnschilders. Van Gerrit Dou tot Frans van Mieris de Jonge 1630–1760* (Zwolle, 1988; English summary)

Smith, David, *Masks of Wedlock: Seventeenth-century Dutch Marriage Portraiture* (Ann Arbor, MI, 1982)

—, 'Towards a Protestant Aesthetics: Rembrandt's 1655 *Sacrifice of Isaac*', *Art History*, III (1985), pp. 290–302

Spies, Marijke, *Arctic Routes to Fabled Lands: Olivier Brunel and the Passage to China and Cathay in the Sixteenth Century*, trans. Myra Heerspink Scholz (Amsterdam, 1997)

Stone-Ferrier, Linda, *Images of Textiles: The Weave of Seventeenth-century Dutch Art and Society* (Ann Arbor, MI, 1985), pp. 1–40

—, 'Rembrandt's Landscape Etchings: Defying Modernity's Encroachment', *Art History*, XV (1992), pp. 403–33

Straten, Roelof van, *Young Rembrandt: The Leiden Years, 1606–1632* (Leiden, 2005)

Strauss, Walter, and Marjon van der Meulen, *The Rembrandt Documents* (New York, 1977)

Sutton, Elizabeth, *Early Modern Dutch Prints of Africa* (Farnham, 2012)

Tummers, Anna, *Frans Hals: Eye to Eye with Rembrandt, Rubens and Titian* (Haarlem, 2013)

Tümpel, Astrid, and Peter Schatborn, *Pieter Lastman: The Man Who Taught Rembrandt* (Zwolle, 1991)

Tümpel, Christian, *Rembrandt: All Paintings in Colour* (Antwerp, 1993)

—, and Astrid Tümpel, *Rembrandt: Images and Metaphors* (London, 2006)

—, *Rembrandt legt die Bibel aus* (Berlin, 1970)

Visser 't Hooft, W. A., *Rembrandt and the Gospel* (New York, 1960)

Waal, H. van de, *Steps toward Rembrandt* (Amsterdam, 1974), esp. pp. 28–72

—, '*The Syndics* and Their Legend', *Oud Holland*, LXXI (1956), pp. 61–107

Welu, James, 'Vermeer: His Cartographic Sources', *Art Bulletin*, LVII
     (1975), pp. 529–47
Westermann, Mariët, *Rembrandt* (London, 2000)
Wetering, Ernst van de, and Barnhard Schnackenburg, eds,
     The Mystery of the Young Rembrandt (Kassel and Amsterdam, 2001)
Wheelock, Arthur, Jr, *Jan Lievens: A Dutch Master Rediscovered*, exh. cat.,
     Washington, National Gallery of Art (Washington, DC, 2009)
—, *Rembrandt's Late Religious Portraits*, exh. cat., Washington, National
     Gallery of Art (Washington, DC, 2005)
—, and Adele Seeff, eds, *The Public and Private in Dutch Culture
     of the Golden Age* (Newark, DE, 2000)
White, Christopher, *Rembrandt* (London, 1984)
—, and Quentin Buvelot, eds, *Rembrandt by Himself*, exh. cat.,
     London, National Gallery; The Hague, Mauritshuis
     (London and The Hague, 1999)
Winkel, Marieke de, *Fashion and Fancy: Dress and Meaning in Rembrandt's
     Paintings* (Amsterdam, 2006)
Zandvliet, Kees, *Mapping for Money: Maps, Plans and Topographic Paintings
     and Their Role in Dutch Overseas Expansion during the 16th and 17th Centuries*
     (Amsterdam, 1998)
—, *The Dutch Encounter with Asia, 1600–1950* (Amsterdam, 2002)
Zell, Michael, *Reframing Rembrandt: Jews and the Christian Image in
     Seventeenth-century Amsterdam* (Berkeley, CA, 2009)

ACKNOWLEDGEMENTS

Every author is the grateful recipient of both direct and indirect assistance, and in the case of Rembrandt studies, the debts are deep and historic. Many are cited in the bibliography, and many others could be added. But while I could never itemize the great predecessors on whose giant shoulders I am privileged to stand, I want to start by acknowledging the wise Nestors of my training, some of whom I was privileged to know personally: Egbert Haverkamp-Begemann, Julius Held, Wolfgang Stechow, Christian Tümpel and in particular my own, lately departed *Doktorvater*, Seymour Slive. Several marvellous Dutch scholars have opened our eyes to much new and wider Rembrandt insight in context, especially Albert Blankert and Eric Jan Sluijter, and for the history of Holland and of Amsterdam and its culture, we all owe great debts to Jonathan Israel, Simon Schama and Steven Nadler.

But in this field, the roll call of contemporaries who have shared the Rembrandt journey across my career needs to be sounded: Clifford Ackley, Ann Jensen Adams, Peter van der Coelen, Barbara Gaehtgens, Amy Golahny, George Keyes, Jürgen Müller, Cynthia Schneider and Linda Stone-Ferrier. An even closer circle of Rembrandt colleagues and great friends have sustained this author over the years, some for almost a half-century: Margaret Carroll, Perry Chapman, Paul Crenshaw, Stephanie Dickey, Gary Schwartz, Mariët Westermann, Arthur Wheelock and Michael Zell. Closest of all are those friends and colleagues who have also been collaborators, particularly Lloyd Dewitt, Aneta Georgievska-Shine and, most significantly and lastingly, Shelley Perlove. This book is dedicated to Shelley in love and gratitude, as the closest offering I can give her instead of the *Festschrift* that she deserves for all that she has contributed to the discipline of art history, both south and north of the Alps, but especially to Rembrandt, across the decades.

But the book has one other dedication: to my family. When one writes a life story of an artist, the importance of his family always stands at the heart of that biography. So it is with this author. My own children, Zachary and Laura, now grown up and with successful careers of their own, have taught as well as humbled me across my own biography. And to their other parent, my wife of four decades, Elizabeth Silver-Schack, I owe the greatest debt – across an entire adult life, then, now and for ever.

PHOTO ACKNOWLEDGEMENTS

The author and publishers wish to express their thanks to the below sources of illustrative material and/or permission to reproduce it. Some locations are given here in the interests of brevity.

The British Museum, London: 49; Frans Hals Museum, Haarlem: 10; Frick Collection, New York: 6; Gemäldegalerie Berlin: 22, 24, 29, 31; Gemäldegalerie Dresden: 41, 53; Huis Oranje-Nassau, The Hague (on long-term loan from the Mauritshuis, The Hague): 37; Isabella Stewart Gardner Museum, Boston: 7; Kenwood House, London: 56; Mauritshuis, The Hague: 9; Metropolitan Museum of Art: 47 (purchase, Rogers Fund, special funds, James S. Deely Gift, and Gift of Edna H. Sachs and other gifts and bequests, by exchange), 50 (Robert Lehman Collection), 52 (purchase, special contributions and funds given or bequeathed by friends of the Museum); Minneapolis Institute of Arts: 46; Musée Jacquemart-Andre, Paris: 38; Musée du Louvre, Paris: 33; Museum Boijmans-Van Beuningen, Rotterdam: 42; Museum of Fine Arts, Boston: 3; Muzeum Narodowe, Warsaw: 44; National Gallery, London: 16, 36; National Gallery of Art, Washington, DC: 1, 2, 59; National Gallery of Victoria, Melbourne: 21; Nationalmuseum, Stockholm: 19; Orange-Nassau Trust, The Hague: 39; photos Pierpont Morgan Library, New York (Department of Drawings and Prints): 5, 13, 14, 15, 23, 25, 26, 27, 30, 32, 48, 54, 55; Rijksmuseum, Amsterdam: 8, 11, 17, 20, 34, 45, 57; Royal Palace, Amsterdam: 18; Six Collection, Amsterdam: 51; Staatliche Museen, Kassel: 12; Städel Kunstinstitut, Frankfurt: 40; State Hermitage Museum, St Petersburg: 35; Wallraf-Richartz Museum, Cologne: 58.

INDEX